**"A TERRIFIC RESOURCE** to maximize the value of your financial adviser."

> JOHN CAMMACK
> Vice President
> T. Rowe Price Associates, Inc.

"'Simplify! Simplify!' exclaimed Henry David Thoreau. That is precisely what Lynn Brenner's *Smart Questions to Ask Your Financial Advisers* does. As more and more Americans seek the advice of professional financial advisers, *Smart Questions to Ask Your Financial Advisers* is **A TIMELY AND VALUABLE RESOURCE FOR CONSUMERS**. It helps consumers intelligently define their goals and **SHOWS THEM HOW TO POSITIVELY COMMUNICATE THEM TO THEIR ADVISERS**."

> RONALD W. ROGÉ, MS, CFP
> R.W. Rogé & Company, Inc.

**"SOLID ADVICE, WRITTEN CLEARLY AND WELL.** *Smart Questions* gives answers to the money management questions you're most likely to ask—**IN A Q&A FORMAT THAT MAKES THE INFORMATION VERY ACCESSIBLE. LYNN BRENNER IS A WINNER**."

> GRACE W. WEINSTEIN
> Personal finance columnist
> *Investor's Business Daily*

SMART
QUESTIONS
TO ASK YOUR

# Financial
# ADVISERS

Also available from
**THE BLOOMBERG PERSONAL BOOKSHELF**

*Smarter Insurance Solutions*
by Janet Bamford

*Investing in Small-Cap Stocks*
by Christopher Graja and Elizabeth Ungar, Ph.D.

*A Commonsense Guide to Your 401(k)*
by Mary Rowland
(December 1997)

*A Commonsense Guide to Mutual Funds*
by Mary Rowland

*Choosing and Using an HMO*
by Ellyn Spragins
(November 1997)

And from
**THE BLOOMBERG PROFESSIONAL LIBRARY**

*Best Practices for Financial Advisors*
by Mary Rowland

*Protecting Your Practice*
by Katherine Vessenes
in cooperation with the IAFP

S M A R T
QUESTIONS
TO ASK YOUR

# Financial
# ADVISERS

## LYNN BRENNER

ICON ILLUSTRATIONS BY MARK MATCHO

BLOOMBERG PRESS
PRINCETON

Books are available for bulk purchases at special discounts. For information, please write: Special Markets Department, Bloomberg Press.

This publication contains the author's opinions and is designed to provide accurate and authoritative information. It is sold with the understanding that the author, publisher, and Bloomberg L.P. are not engaged in rendering legal, accounting, investment-planning, or other professional advice. The reader should seek the services of a qualified professional for such advice; the author, publisher, and Bloomberg L.P. cannot be held responsible for any loss incurred as a result of specific investments or planning decisions made by the reader.

First edition published 1997
1  3  5  7  9  10  8  6  4  2

Brenner, Lynn

    Smart questions to ask your financial advisers / Lynn Brenner.

       p.   cm. - - (Bloomberg personal bookshelf)

    Includes index.

    ISBN 1-57660-015-7

    1.   Finance, Personal.    I. Title.    II. Series.

HG179.B72728   1997

332.024—dc21                        97-29575

                                          CIP

Icon illustrations by Mark Matcho.

Book design by Don Morris Design

*To Susan Maxwell,*

*my best friend*

— L . B .

# ACKNOWLEDGMENTS

MANY WONDERFUL PEOPLE helped to make this book possible.

My heartfelt thanks to *Newsday*'s readers, who for the past eight years have written to the Family Finance column with questions about every kind of financial dilemma, and to the financial advisers who have generously taken the time to help me answer those questions. They inspired this book.

I am deeply indebted to the dedicated team of professionals at Bloomberg Press whose skills helped to shape, edit, design, and illustrate the book, and bring it to your attention: Jared Kieling, Steven Gittelson, Barbara Diez, Don Morris, Josh Klenert, Mark Matcho, John Crutcher, Lisa Goetz, Priscilla Treadwell, Karen Cook, Jack Flynn, and Christina Palumbo.

Finally, I want to thank members of my family: my sister and brother, Nina Bernstein and Paul Bernstein, who in between meeting their own deadlines are always willing to pinch hit as researchers; my husband, Gerald McKelvey, without whom I could never have set up the computer on which this book was written; and my daughter, Nora McKelvey, who is a constant source of joy and moral support.

# INTRODUCTION

ERSONAL FINANCE books typically give broad answers to common questions. The general information they provide can be very useful. But when you need specific answers that fit your own situation, you don't open a book—you go to a financial planner, or a tax accountant, or a lawyer.

This book tells you what to ask when you get there.

You don't need an in-depth understanding of the financial markets or even a passing familiarity with investment jargon—let alone the intricacies of tax law or insurance regulation—to talk intelligently to a professional adviser.

But you do need to ask the right questions to get advice that's truly responsive to your needs—advice that helps you to invest well, to take advantage of all the available tax breaks, and to avoid costly financial mistakes. In fact, after covering personal finance and business for more than 20 years, I'm convinced that knowing what to ask is all that separates the smart shoppers from the naive ones.

This book gives you key questions to ask in eight major areas of personal finance—investing, negotiating prenuptial and divorce agreements, buying/owning/selling a house, buying insurance, coping with the loss of a job, estate planning, tax planning, and retirement planning.

It explains why each question is important and tells you how a good adviser will analyze the relevant issues to come up with an answer that fits your needs.

Some questions are appropriately directed to two types of adviser. If you're contemplating divorce, for example, you can save yourself a lot of money and grief by consulting a tax accountant as well as lawyers and/or a mediator. Other questions can be handled by any of several different advisers; you could consult either a tax accountant or a financial planner about the advisability of tax-exempt investments, for instance. The icons accompanying each question tell you which advisers to consult, as shown below:

 **Financial planner**

 **Insurance agent**

 **Lawyer**

 **Stockbroker**

 **Tax accountant**

Since every financial salesperson now calls himself a financial planner, a definition is in order: When I say a financial planner, I mean a person who is trained to advise you on a broad range of financial subjects, including investing, taxes, insurance, estate and retirement planning—and who is paid for his advice by you, not by companies whose products he recommends.

At the back of the book, you'll find an epilogue that tells you what professional credentials to look for and what kinds of questions to ask in order to find financial advisers who are both knowledgeable and honest.

One last thought: No matter how good your advisers, the final decisions must always be yours. Nobody else knows your needs as well as you do, or cares as much about satisfying them. With good advice, you can become your own best financial planner.

**CHAPTER**

1

# INVESTING

NVESTMENT ADVICE HAS never been as readily available as it is today. But most of this advice is free, which means it's designed to serve the adviser's needs, not yours. Free advice is just a sophisticated form of product marketing.

Financial salespeople are trained and paid to sell products, not to analyze your financial needs. However wise it sounds, their free "advice" boils down to a pitch to buy whatever they're selling, whether it's stocks, bonds, insurance, annuities, or mutual funds.

A real financial planner's job is to help you figure out where you stand financially, to design a cost-effective strategy to meet your short- and long-term goals, and to recommend investments that fit the strategy.

When you want disinterested advice about what kinds of investments will fit your needs, go to a financial planner whom you pay by fee only. Go to a stockbroker or an insurance agent when you want to buy stocks, bonds, or insurance.

*(For information on how to find a financial planner who is both objective and competent, see "Epilogue.")*

## Q1 What should I invest in to meet my goals?

There are no one-size-fits-all investments.

No financial planner worth his salt will suggest any product without finding out how soon you need this money, how much and how frequently you expect to add to the investment between now and then, and what you plan to do with it. Be prepared to describe your hopes, dreams, and investment objectives. The more detail you can muster, the better. Are you building an emergency fund? Saving for a trip to Disney World next year? Investing for a college education 15 years in the future, or a comfortable retirement in 30 years?

Investing without specific goals is like trying to pack a suitcase for an unknown destination. If you're going on a midwinter business trip to Buffalo, you don't pack Bermuda shorts, no matter how stylish they are—and if you're saving for next summer's vacation, you don't invest in a growth-stock fund even if it has a great track record.

Ask your adviser to explain his or her recommendations. What makes this type of investment appropriate for your goal? What alternative products might you also consider? Why does the adviser think this particular investment is the best fit, given your goal?

Bear in mind that there are only two basic categories of investment: you can lend your money and earn interest on it in investments like CDs or money market funds or bonds; or you can buy an asset (like stocks, real estate, or gold coins) that you hope will grow in value so you can sell it at a profit. There are many investments in both these categories, each with its own advantages and disadvantages.

Money market funds give you principal stability and instant access to your money, for example: the value of your account won't go down, and you can draw on it anytime. But money market funds don't pay much. Bonds give you a steady, predictable income stream, but their fixed payments are vulnerable to inflation; and if interest rates go up, your bond loses value. Stocks promise the best long-term growth, but they have the greatest short-term volatility. Over a 10-year period, a stock investment can easily triple in value; over a one-year period, its value might be cut in half.

Intelligent investing is largely a matter of matching these characteristics to your own goals. Money market funds make sense for an emergency account, where stability and access to your money are more important than high return. After you retire, predictable income may be a greater priority than long-term growth, making bonds more attractive. In an account you won't tap for 25 years, long-term growth is much more important than steady income or liquidity, so stocks are the investment of choice.

**NOTE:** Don't just rely on your instincts to tell you which investments are risky and which are safe. Ask your adviser to explain the relative risk of each investment in connection with your specific goal. It's as risky to put all your retirement money into "safe" bond funds that can't protect you from inflation as it is to use your emergency cash to chase hot stock tips.

Of course, you don't want investments that turn you into a nail-biting insomniac, either. So here's a sensible method for limiting risk: Assume that at the worst, the stock market will temporarily lose half its value, says Larry Elkin, a financial planner and tax accountant in Hastings-on-Hudson, New York. If you can't handle more than a 30 percent temporary decline in the total value of your long-term investments, no more than 60 percent of your long-term portfolio should be in stocks.

## Q2 How can I expect this investment to behave?

"Don't worry, it will make you rich" is not a good answer. How will it make money for you? How could it lose money? What are the best- and worst-case scenarios? If your adviser says there is no worst-case scenario, you need another adviser. There's a worst case for every investment.

Ask your adviser to show you the investment's total

return—minus all fees and expenses—for the past three-, five-, and 10-year periods, compared with an appropriate benchmark *(see "Appendix" for a list of standard benchmarks)*. The performance data should come from an independent third party like Morningstar, Value Line, or Lipper Analytical Services.

Ask how the investment normally behaves under different economic conditions: rising interest rates, falling interest rates, high inflation, a recession, a bull market, a bear market.

**NOTE:** The more clearly defined a mutual fund's investment objective and strategy, the easier it is to predict how the fund is likely to behave in different environments. One reason to avoid mutual funds whose managers are allowed to invest in almost anything is that you can't draw their risk profile.

You need this information to understand what you're buying and to build a diversified portfolio. You want investments that behave differently in each economic environment. That way, you minimize the risk that they'll all be clobbered at the same time.

**NOTE:** Avoid any adviser who claims he or she can keep moving your money into the optimum investment for each economic environment. *Nobody—professional or amateur—has ever timed the market successfully on a consistent basis.*

## GENERAL GUIDELINES

◆ An expanding economy with moderate inflation and low interest rates is good for both stocks and bonds.

◆ When interest rates rise, bonds lose value, because nobody pays full value for an old bond when for the same price he can buy a new one that yields more. Rising interest rates are also bad for stocks: As rates go up, investors move their money out of the stock market into interest-paying investments like money market funds, new CDs, and new bonds.

◆ Short periods of high inflation are bad for the stock
market; but over periods of a decade or longer,
stocks have outperformed inflation by a wide margin. When you own stocks, you own a share of corporate profits—and in the long run, corporations
beat inflation by passing rising costs along to their
customers. Cash and fixed-income investments (i.e.,
money market funds, CDs, Treasuries, bonds) perform very badly against long-term inflation. According to Chicago research firm Ibbotson Associates,
from 1926 through 1996, stocks have outpaced inflation by 7.6 percent a year. By contrast, corporate
bonds have beaten inflation by 2.5 percent a year,
government bonds by 2 percent a year, and cash
investments by just 0.6 percent a year. And those
gains are before taxes.

◆ Recessions (times of high consumer debt, rising
unemployment, shrinking demand for products) are
bad for the stock market in general—but the stocks of
companies in consumer-staples businesses like food,
health care, and pharmaceuticals perform better than
those of companies in cyclical industries like housing,
automobile, steel, and paper.

◆ Falling interest rates are very good for bonds and
bond funds because investors pay a premium for old
bonds that yield more than new issues. Falling rates
are also good for stocks, because investors move their
money from lower-yielding CDs and money market
funds into the stock market.

◆ Mortgage-backed bonds like Ginnie Maes are particularly sensitive to interest rates. Like all bonds, they
lose value when rates rise. They also lose value when
interest rates fall, because homeowners refinance the
mortgages underlying your Ginnie Mae investment.
The result: Your principal is repaid and must be reinvested at the prevailing lower rate.

◆ A long period of deflation like the Great Depression is very bad for both stocks and bonds. The best-

performing investment in a depression is the highest quality fixed-income instrument available: U.S. Treasuries.

**NOTE:** Before buying any mutual fund, ask your adviser how it has performed in past bull and bear markets. Funds that excel in bull markets tend to underperform in bear markets, and vice versa. It makes sense to own both kinds.

### Q3 What kind of return should I expect from this investment?

Get ready to be disappointed.

A six-year bull market (late 1990 through mid-1997, still going strong as I write) has given most investors—including many professionals who ought to know better—the euphoric expectation that 15 percent to 20 percent annual returns are normal.

Forget it.

Since 1926 the stock market has delivered a 10.7 percent average annual compound return, according to Ibbotson Associates. But remember, this historic return is just a long-term average, in which the up and down years are balanced out. The stock market's year-to-year ride has been very bumpy. Annual returns have soared as high as 53 percent and dropped as much as 43 percent. Most of the time, they've fluctuated between a gain of 30 percent and a loss of 10 percent.

Historically, the stock market has averaged one down year every three years. Before buying any investment, ask your adviser to give you its year-to-year history as well as its long-term average return. That way, you'll know what to expect along the way.

## Q4 What will this investment cost me—in commissions, management fees, and administrative and marketing expenses?

There are three important things to remember about expenses:

**1** They always reduce your return.

**2** Unlike investment performance, they are totally predictable.

**3** They vary dramatically among otherwise indistinguishable investments.

**NOTE:** Cutting your costs is the only foolproof way to boost your return without taking any additional risk.

Ask your financial adviser to tell you the total cost of any investment you're considering—*including, but not limited to, his or her sales commission*—and to show you how it compares to the average cost of similar products.

When you're considering a mutual fund, ask your adviser to tell you its annual expense ratio; whether or not there's a 12b-1 fee (which pays the fund's marketing expenses), and if so, how much it is; whether or not it carries a front load or a back load; and what its annual turnover is. Turnover shows how often the fund buys and sells assets. A fund with a 100 percent turnover rate has replaced its total portfolio within a 12-month period. The average U.S. stock fund has an 83 percent turnover rate. Aggressive growth funds typically have a higher turnover rate than conservative value funds. But bear in mind that every time a fund buys or sells assets, it incurs brokerage commissions and trading costs. So the higher a fund's turnover rate, the higher its general operating expenses—and the better its performance must be to overcome those expenses.

The expense ratio shows a mutual fund's annual expenses as a percentage of its assets under management. The average U.S. stock fund has a 1.44 percent expense ratio, according to Morningstar. This means the fund's investment return is reduced by 1.44 percent every year to cover its costs. (The expense ratio has already been deducted from results printed in newspapers and shareholder statements.)

The expense ratio does not include any sales charges or commissions (i.e., loads) you may pay to buy fund shares; nor does it include the fund's brokerage and trading expenses, a cost that's passed to shareholders. Annual turnover is a good guide to these transaction fees *(see above)*.

ACCORDING TO MORNINGSTAR, all mutual funds charge the following fees:

◆ Annual investment management fees that can range from 0.01 percent to 2.5 percent of fund assets.

◆ Annual administrative fees ranging from 0.0015 percent to 1.5 percent of fund assets.

Some funds also charge:

◆ An annual 12b-1 fee ranging from 0.01 percent to 0.75 percent of fund assets. This covers the cost of marketing the fund to new customers. Some 'no-load' funds pay brokers' sales commissions with 12b-1 fees.

◆ A front load. This is a sales commission you pay to buy shares. It can range from 0.4 percent to 9 percent of your investment. (*Note:* You may pay a load even if you buy a fund directly from the fund company over the telephone.)

◆ A back-end load, which is a sales commission charged when you sell shares. It ranges from 0.05 percent to 5.5 percent of your investment, and typically declines for about four years until it disappears.

Sometimes the same fund sells several types of shares: "A" shares are front-loaded. "B" shares are back-loaded, and usually have higher 12b-1 fees than

"A" shares. "C" shares have no load—but their annual 12b-1 fees are higher still, so they can actually cost more than a one-time load.

**NOTE:** Many stellar mutual funds don't charge loads or 12b-1 fees. Stick with them.

Load funds don't perform any better than no-load funds—and they start you with a handicap. If you pay a 4 percent load on a fund that has 1.5 percent operating expenses, for example, you must earn 5.5 percent in the first year *just to break even.* A terrific manager may more than overcome a load; then again, he may not. Past performance is history. The manager who built a great track record may not do as well in future—or he may quit after you invest in the fund.

**NOTE:** Annual expenses make as much difference to your return as loads: A 1994 Morningstar study divided U.S. stock funds into four groups based on their average annual expenses from 1983 through 1993. The group with the lowest expenses returned *1.9 percent more a year* during that decade than the group with the highest expenses.

**NOTE:** In a bond fund, lower expenses often mean lower risk. If two bond funds have the same yield but different expense ratios, the one with higher expenses is taking more risk.

HOW MUCH SHOULD YOU PAY? Certainly not more than industry-average annual expense ratios—and less, if you can. The average figures supplied by Morningstar:
◆ U.S. stock fund                   1.44 percent
◆ International stock fund           1.86 percent
◆ Emerging markets fund             2.10 percent
◆ Investment grade bond fund        0.92 percent
◆ High yield bond fund              1.36 percent
◆ Municipal bond fund               1.01 percent

**NOTE:** It costs extra to have a financial planner or broker manage a mutual fund portfolio for you—i.e., choose funds and monitor their performance. If you feel the additional expense is warranted, buy this service from a fee-only planner who invests in no-load, no 12b-1 fee funds, and charges not more than 1 percent of assets a year as a management fee.

*(For information on insurance product expenses, see* **Q14***, this chapter, and "Insurance," **Q1***.)*

## Q5 Do my investments work well as a combination?

One of the most valuable services a financial planner can perform is to look at your portfolio as a whole.

Asset allocation—how your money is divided among stocks, bonds, cash, and real estate—is what drives your investment return. Getting the proportions right, and keeping them right, is much more important than picking the very best stock or bond fund. Think of your portfolio as an omelet: Average ingredients in the right proportions make a much better dish than great ingredients in the wrong proportions. An omelet that's one-third first-rate salt and two-thirds top-quality eggs would taste terrible.

The right investment mix can boost your potential return *without* increasing your risk of loss.

For example, foreign stocks and small company stocks have higher long-term returns than blue-chip stocks; they're also riskier. But when you combine all three, you get the upside without the downside: A portfolio of blue chips, small caps, and foreign stocks has a higher potential return than a portfolio of blue chips alone—with no greater degree of risk.

Asset allocation works by combining investments that don't normally move in tandem. That increases the likelihood that you'll have at least one investment performing well in every economic environment, boosting your overall return.

A good financial adviser will analyze your asset allocation by listing everything you own—your house, your Individual Retirement Accounts, 401(k) accounts, bank accounts, and brokerage holdings—and calculating the percentage of your total assets in each broad category, before telling you how your allocation can be improved to reduce your risk and increase your potential return.

Example: A 52-year-old single woman earns $50,000 a year. She owns a $200,000 house. She has $92,000 in an international stock fund, $25,000 in a growth-and-income fund, $48,000 in a municipal bond fund with long average maturity, and $10,000 in a tax-free money market fund. The funds all have good track records. What's wrong with this portfolio?

Well, excluding the house, 52 percent of her assets are invested in an international fund, says Lewis Altfest, a New York City financial planner. A better mix would be to keep 65 percent of her money in stocks, but divide it among international stocks (20 percent), big company stocks (40 percent), mid-sized company stocks (20 percent), and small company stocks (20 percent). "She can keep about 35 percent of her assets in bonds and cash," adds Altfest, "and in her tax bracket, munis make sense. But I'd reduce risk by transferring more than one-third of those long-term muni holdings into a short-to-intermediate muni fund."

Obviously, optimal asset allocation depends on your specific situation, but here are some rules of thumb:

◆ **You're never too old for stocks.** When you retire at 65, you can expect to live another 20 to 30 years. You still need growth investments to outpace inflation.

◆ **A good U.S. stock allocation should include growth stocks, income-paying stocks (sometimes called value** stocks), and small company stocks.

◆ At least 10 percent of a well-balanced portfolio should be in foreign stocks for diversification.

◆ Long-term bonds and bond funds are a mistake for most investors. They pay higher interest than short-term bonds, but they're much riskier; as interest rates rise, their value plummets. "Over the past 70 years, long-term bonds haven't paid investors for the additional risk they represent," says Scott Lummer, managing director of Ibbotson Associates. For diversification with minimal interest rate risk, stick with bonds or bond funds that mature in five years or less.

◆ For most individual investors, owning a house is sufficient real estate exposure. If you want additional real estate investments, Lummer advises investing no more than 5 percent to 10 percent of your long-term portfolio in REIT mutual funds—funds that invest in real estate investment trusts.

**NOTE:** The key to asset allocation is maintaining it. If you keep tinkering with the mix, you'll sell investments that are performing poorly and buy those that are doing well. In other words, you'll sell low and buy high—a sure way to lose money.

Ask your adviser to help you rebalance your portfolio every year by selling investments in an asset class that performed well and buying them in a class that lagged. Let's say you start with a 75/20/5 mix of stocks, bonds, and cash, for example; your stocks soar, your bonds lag, and a year later, the mix is 85/10/5. To rebalance, sell stocks and invest the proceeds in bonds.

**NOTE:** Don't rebalance without considering transaction costs and tax consequences. In taxable accounts, you may prefer to direct new money into underperforming asset classes without selling existing investments.

**NOTE:** Don't expect an 'asset allocation fund' to do your rebalancing for you. Most of these funds invest in a mix of stocks, bonds, and cash, but typically keep changing their allocations in an attempt to time the market. This is called 'tactical' asset allocation; the results can be disastrous.

### Q6 Does it make sense for me to buy individual securities instead of stock mutual funds?

Not unless you have:

**1** At least $500,000 to invest in stocks, *and*

**2** The time and ability to pick and monitor some 25 or 30 stocks in diversified industries, *or*

**3** The expertise to assess a broker's recommendations.

Individual stocks give you one big advantage over stock funds: You decide when to sell a stock, so you control when you'll pay taxes on any increase in its value. In a mutual fund, the portfolio manager decides what to sell, and when—and the fund's taxable gains are automatically passed to its shareholders.

But it takes a substantial portfolio of individual securities to achieve the diversification and low trading costs and professional portfolio management that are available in a mutual fund for a single $2,000 investment. You may want to buy individual stocks *in addition* to stock funds, however, if:

**1** You have ongoing professional information about specific companies or industries that will help you make better-than-average stock picks; *or*

**2** You find stock picking interesting and fun and will therefore devote leisure time to doing your own research; *or*

**3** You're savvy enough to judge your broker's recommendations—and confident enough to reject them when you disagree with him.

If you don't fit any of these categories, stick with

mutual funds.

When you buy a stock, *you're buying a company.* An adviser who recommends a stock should tell you what the company does, where it stands in its industry, and most important, where its future growth will come from. Why is it a good buy? Are its earnings growing faster than those of others in its industry? Is its stock selling at a bargain price? Does it pay high dividends? If you're too shy to ask your broker for this information, you have the wrong broker.

**NOTE:** If you buy individual securities, you should read *Value Line Investment Survey,* a newsletter available at most public libraries—even if you have a great broker. *Value Line* provides constantly updated information about more than 1,700 stocks.

**NOTE:** Don't invest heavily in the company and/or industry that pays your salary, or you'll be putting your job and your investments in one basket.

**NOTE:** Stocks are a *long term* investment. "All my great stocks came through in the second, third, fourth, fifth year—not the first," said Peter Lynch, the great stock picker who ran Fidelity's Magellan fund for 13 years. "Your broker will call after the stock doubles and say, 'Sell and buy something else' —that's how he earns commissions. If you own a stock nine years and it grows tenfold, you've made a lot, but the broker has made zip."

**NOTE:** You can buy stocks without a broker. More than 200 U.S. companies now sell their stock directly to investors. For a list of stocks you can buy directly, write to *DRIP Investor,* a newsletter that covers dividend-reinvestment plans, at 7412 Calumet Ave., Suite 200, Hammond, IN 46324-2692. You'll also find a list of no-load stocks on the Internet, at Netstock Direct's Web site (www.netstockdirect.com).

**Q7** **Do I need fixed-income investments? And if I do, which make more sense for me, bonds or bond mutual funds?**

Some fixed-income investments make sense even in a portfolio whose main goal is aggressive growth; the dividend income they pay helps to cushion stock market losses.

But there are probably more misconceptions about bonds than any other investment. Most investors don't realize that:

**1** Bonds are volatile. Their value drops when interest rates rise—and the longer the bond's maturity, the bigger the drop. "Think of it as a seesaw, with interest rates on one end and bond prices on the other end," says Michael Ross, a Smithtown, New York, financial planner. "The further towards the end of the seesaw you are—the longer your bond's maturity—the bigger the moves up and down. The closer you are to the middle of the seesaw—the shorter your bond's maturity—the less you move up and down."

**2** There's a big difference between bonds and bond funds. With the exception of Treasuries, individual bonds are prohibitively expensive unless you can invest about $50,000 at a clip. Here's why: There's no central bond market comparable to the stock market; you buy bonds from a dealer's inventory and the price you pay includes his markup. The smaller the purchase, the bigger the markup. Any purchase under $100,000 is considered small.

The advantage of buying individual bonds is that you control their credit quality and you can tailor their maturities to your needs. If you hold good quality bonds to maturity, you'll get your original investment back; in the meantime you have predictable income. If you build a 'ladder' of bonds—buying them in a succession of one-year maturities going out 10 years, for example—you'll have cash coming in every year to reinvest at prevailing rates.

The downside: If you must sell a bond before it matures, and interest rates have risen or the bond issuer's credit rating has fallen since you bought it, you'll take a loss. A very simple example: You buy a $5,000 bond that pays 10 percent or $500. If the prevailing rate rises to 11 percent, you can't sell that bond for $5,000. It's worth only $4,545 because that's all a buyer needs to invest at 11 percent to earn $500.

When you buy an old bond, you pay a premium or a discount, depending on how current interest rates have affected its value. (Before buying a bond, always ask about its yield-to-maturity—the current yield, adjusted to reflect the premium or discount you will pay.)

When you invest in a bond fund, you get immediate diversification. You're buying a share in an entire portfolio of bonds for as little as $2,000 or $3,000. You also get professional management, lower trading costs (the fund manager is less likely than an individual investor to get soaked for huge markups), and liquidity. Selling mutual fund shares is much easier and less expensive than selling individual bonds.

But you won't have predictable income or the assurance that you'll get back your principal if you wait long enough. Both your interest income and the value of your shares will fluctuate constantly, as the fund buys and sells bonds. There's nothing fixed about fixed-income funds.

**NOTE:** The two important things in a bond fund are total return—the fund's yield, plus or minus changes in its share price—and annual expenses. *Always ask for a bond fund's annual expenses compared to the average expenses for bond funds in the same category.* Expenses can range from as little as 0.25 percent to more than 1.70 percent of fund assets. The lower they are, the bigger your return.

**NOTE:** When interest rates are low, it's tempting to buy the highest-yielding bond fund. *Don't do it*. The only way a fund can achieve higher yield when rates are low is to buy lower-quality or longer-maturity bonds. Those are the very bonds that will tank when interest rates rise—and when rates are low, they're likelier to rise than to fall.

**NOTE:** If you want bonds mainly to diversify a stock port-folio, stick with bond funds whose average maturity is under five years.

**NOTE:** If you want safety and predictable income, but can't afford individual bonds, build a ladder (i.e., a succession of maturities) of CDs or U.S. Treasuries. You can buy Treasuries directly from the Federal Reserve for no sales charge, or from a bank or broker.

I think a ladder of CDs or Treasuries is a better invest-ment than unit investment trusts, which are often promoted as a low-cost alternative to individual bonds.

UITs are $1,000 shares in a fixed portfolio of bonds that are supposed to be held until maturity. As a UIT owner, you receive regular income payments—your share of the portfolio's earnings and return of princi-pal as its bonds mature.

The negatives:

◆ **UIT income isn't really fixed**, because the underly-ing portfolio often includes callable bonds—i.e., bonds that can be redeemed early by their issuers.

◆ **UITs have no performance record**. They aren't mon-itored by third parties like Morningstar or Lipper Ana-lytical Services. They're sometimes a dumping ground for poor quality bonds.

◆ **UITs are expensive, considering that they're shares in an unmanaged portfolio**. You pay a 4 percent or 5 percent sales commission, plus an annual administra-tive fee, and sometimes a surrender fee as well.

## Q8 How will my mutual fund gains be taxed?

Taxes on fund profits are often an unpleasant surprise. Ask your adviser about tax consequences before selling shares.

You'll owe taxes on fund profits every year, whether you sell shares or not, unless you own the fund in a tax-deferred account like an IRA or a 401(k) plan. Mutual funds pass their annual earnings to their shareholders. You must pay taxes on these distributions, even if you automatically reinvest them in additional fund shares.

And of course, when you sell mutual fund shares, you'll owe taxes on any profit over your original cost. Under the 1997 tax law, your profit when you sell shares you've owned for 12 months or less is still taxable at ordinary income tax rates. Calculating the tax on shares you owned for more than 12 months and sold in May, June, and July of 1997 is anything but simple: The profit on shares that you sold between May 7 and July 28 and owned for more than 12 months is taxed at a top rate of 20 percent. But from July 29 on, your profit on shares owned for more than 12 months but not more than 18 months is taxed at a top rate of 28 percent. From July 29 on, the profit on shares you've owned for more than 18 months is taxed at a top rate of 20 percent.

If your ordinary income tax rate is 15 percent, your long-term capital gains rate on assets held more than 18 months is 10 percent.

Starting in 2001, profit on shares bought after 2000 and owned for more than five years will be taxable at a top rate of 18 percent. If your ordinary income tax rate is 15 percent, your profit on these shares will be taxed at 8 percent.

Just to make your life more complicated, the federal

government isn't the only entity taxing capital gains. The states impose capital gains taxes, too—and some states don't define long-term and short-term gains the same way as the federal government. (This is why you have a tax adviser.)

When you sell shares, you owe taxes on the difference between your original purchase price (known in tax jargon as your cost basis) and the sale proceeds. Let's say you originally invested $1,000, and over time you reinvested an additional $800 in dividends. Then you sell the entire fund for $2,000. What's your profit?

If you think it's $1,000—the $2,000 sale price minus your initial $1,000 investment—you're wrong. Your true cost includes that $800 of reinvested dividends as well as the $1,000 initial investment. Your taxable profit is only $200—$2,000 minus $1,800.

**NOTE:** You or your adviser must keep track of your reinvested dividends so you can add them to your cost basis when you sell the fund—or you'll wind up paying tax on this money twice. Save all your year-end fund statements. They show all your transactions, including the price of shares you bought with additional investments and reinvested dividends.

If you sell all your shares at once, you're taxed on the difference between your total investment and the sale proceeds. But what if you sell only some of your shares? What with periodic purchases and reinvested dividends, you've bought shares at many different prices. What's the original cost of the shares you're selling?

The IRS currently gives you two basic ways to answer this question: You can assume you're selling shares in the order you bought them, using the chronological cost basis recorded in your statements; or you can calculate an average cost per share, regardless of when they were purchased.

For mind-numbing detail on how to do these calculations, read Internal Revenue publication 564, *Mutual Fund Distributions*. Alternatively, hand your year-end fund statements to your tax accountant and pay him or her to do the calculation for you. (If you're lucky, the mutual fund company will do it for you. Some big fund companies automatically run these calculations for shareholders every year.)

WAYS TO MINIMIZE mutual fund tax trauma:

◆ *Don't* write checks on your mutual fund accounts. Every time you write a check, you sell shares and realize a gain or a loss you'll have to report on your tax return. If you want to tap your funds for income, take the distributions in cash instead of reinvesting them.

◆ *Don't* trade a lot in a taxable account. Switching money from one mutual fund to another is as easy as picking up the phone—but every switch is a taxable transaction.

◆ *Don't* buy a mutual fund for a taxable account in November or December before finding out the date on which it distributes its annual capital gains to shareholders. If you buy the day before, as a shareholder of record you're immediately presented with a tax bill. Say you buy 2,000 shares at $10 each. The fund declares a $1 per share dividend the next day. The official share price drops to $9 and the extra $1 per share is considered a taxable distribution. You owe taxes on $2,000, whether you leave it in the fund or not.

◆ *Do* sell all your shares in a fund at one time instead of in stages if they're in a taxable account. If you're a retiree and need to sell shares regularly for income, do it once a year and put the proceeds in a money market fund. You can write checks on a money market account without incurring any capital gain or loss because money market funds maintain a stable $1 per share value.

## Q9 How much money should I keep in a stable, liquid account for emergencies?

It depends on how many breadwinners there are in your family and on your access to relatively low-cost credit.

The conventional wisdom is that everyone needs an emergency account equal to about six months' living expenses. But you can probably get away with only three months' worth if you and your spouse both have secure jobs, or if you could borrow against a home equity line of credit, or if you own a significant sum in stocks and bonds that you could sell if necessary—provided they're held in a taxable account. If you're under age 59 and a half, there's a 10 percent penalty as well as income taxes on any amount you withdraw from a tax-deferred account.

Your investment goal for emergency money is liquidity and safety, not a great return. Use money market funds, which provide quick access to your cash and are also an excellent hedge against short-term inflation: Their interest payments rise or fall with prevailing rates. You'd earn higher interest in a long-term bond fund, but if prevailing rates went up, the value of your shares would plummet.

## Q10 How should my spouse and I coordinate our 401(k)s?

Treat your two 401(k) plans as one portfolio to maximize your investment return.

Ideally, a retirement portfolio should include good mutual funds in four basic stock categories—growth, growth-and-income, small company, and international—and a short-to-intermediate corporate bond fund. Chances are you'll need two 401(k) plans to achieve this broad a mix; many plans don't yet offer a small company fund or an international fund.

If you can't fully fund both 401(k)s, give first priority to the one with the biggest employer match, second place to the plan with better investments. A 50 percent match is an immediate, risk-free 50 percent return on your money—handsome compensation for a mediocre investment line-up.

But double-check how long it will take to become vested in the matching contributions. By law, you must be fully vested after seven years; but some companies start vesting after the third year, while others don't begin until you've participated in the plan for five years. A great match isn't worth anything if you're likely to leave the job before you own it.

**NOTE:** If your employer matches your contributions in company stock, fine. But don't make the very common mistake of using your own contributions to buy company stock, too. "It's risking your family's financial future to have your job and your retirement invested in one company," says Jonathan Pond, president of Financial Planning Information in Boston. "If you think it's a great company, don't buy it for your 401(k) account—buy shares at 85 cents on the dollar in the company stock purchase plan."

### Q11 How should my spouse and I coordinate a 401(k) and a 457 plan? How about a 401(k) and a 403(b) plan?

In general, a 401(k) is the best of these retirement plans, but (naturally) there are exceptions. Depending on your investment goals and on the plan features, there are situations in which you may want to give priority to a 403(b) or a 457.

A 457 plan is used by governments and municipalities, and a 403(b) by public schools, hospitals, churches, and universities. Most other employers sponsor 401(k) plans. All three plans let you save part of your salary through payroll deduction. You pay no taxes on the money you save or on its earnings until you start taking withdrawals, typically after you retire. And with a few exceptions, all three plans forbid withdrawals before you leave your job.

You can roll money from a 401(k) or a 403(b) into an IRA when you leave the job, or into a new employer's 401(k) or 403(b) plan.

A 457 plan isn't a retirement plan. You can't roll it into an IRA or another plan. But there's no 10 percent early withdrawal penalty for tapping the money before age 59 and a half. When you leave your job, you typically have three options: you can withdraw your money in a lump sum and pay taxes on it; take taxable installment withdrawals; or leave it in the plan earning a tax-deferred return until a future date. You don't *have* to start withdrawing it until age 70 and a half.

The annual limit on 401(k) and 403(b) contributions currently is $9,500; on 457 contributions, it's $7,500. In a 401(k), your contribution is often matched by your employer; only about half of 403(b)s provide an employer match; 457 plans don't include any match.

403(b) plans provide the biggest investment selection. In 1996, these plans on average offered 23 mutual funds and 8 annuity contracts—versus just seven funds for the average 401(k). Another 403(b) advantage: If the employer hasn't contributed to the plan, you can often transfer your accumulated savings, while still in the same job, into any investments you choose—even if they aren't on the plan menu. (The downside: Transfers can be expensive; sometimes 403(b) menu investments carry hefty surrender charges.)

Neither 401(k) nor 403(b) money is subject to the claims of your employer's creditors. That will also be true of 457 plan money starting in 1999. Until then, your savings in a 457 won't be legally differentiated from your employer's assets until you withdraw them. That means if the employer goes bankrupt, you could find yourself waiting in line for your savings with other creditors. (This has never happened, however.)

## Q12 Do tax-free investments make sense for me?

It depends on your tax bracket.

Too many people assume municipal bonds must be a great investment because rich people buy them, not realizing that municipal bonds don't make anybody rich.

Rich people buy municipal bonds to minimize their taxes. If you're in a 39.6 percent marginal tax bracket, a 4.5 percent tax-free return is like a 7.45 percent taxable return. To someone in the 15 percent bracket, the same 4.5 percent tax-free return is only the equivalent of a 5.29 percent taxable return.

Municipal bond interest is federally tax-free, and free of state and local taxes to residents of the municipality. That always sounds enticing. But if you're in a low tax bracket, ask your adviser how much you'd earn in Treasuries instead. It might be more. Treasuries are free of state and local taxes, and they're also safer than municipal bonds.

Another advantage of Treasuries is that unlike munibonds, they aren't callable. A callable bond can be redeemed before its scheduled maturity date. Issuers call their bonds for the same reason you refinance your mortgage: to take advantage of lower rates. When your bonds are called you must reinvest in a lower-rate environment.

**NOTE:** Don't sell a tax-free bond without first asking your adviser whether you'll trigger a tax bill. The interest these bonds pay is tax-free, but if you sell a bond for more than you paid, you'll have a taxable capital gain. A bond mutual fund's capital gains, for example, are taxable to its shareholders.

DON'T BUY A TAX-FREE investment unless:
**1** It pays you better than a taxable investment of similar credit quality and maturity, *and*
**2** Your goal is current income. Munis aren't designed to grow your money.

**NOTE:** Don't forget to factor expenses into any comparison of tax-advantaged and taxable products. Many tax-advantaged investments, like variable annuities and life insurance, are horrendously expensive *(see* **Q14**, *and "Insurance,"* **Q1** *and* **Q10**).

## Q13 Does it make sense for me to set up a custodial account for my child's college costs?

It depends on:
**1** Your tax bracket;
**2** Whether or not your child is likely to qualify for need-based financial aid to college; *and*
**3** Your gut reaction at the prospect of making a no-strings six-figure gift to an 18-year-old.

Custodial accounts are owned by children. If you're in a higher tax bracket than your kids, putting money in their names is a good way to reduce the tax bite on college savings. But there is a downside: You can't take the money back. As custodian, you can spend it only on the child's behalf. And she gains control of the account as soon as she reaches legal majority. Also, the fact that she has money in her own name may reduce her eligibility for financial aid, including low-cost college loans.

To set up a custodial account under the Uniform Gift to Minors Act or the Uniform Transfer to Minors Act, all you need do is fill out a one-page form available at any bank, brokerage, insurance, or mutual fund company—and start depositing money.

In 1997, the first $650 of income earned in the account is tax-free. In other words, assuming an 8 percent annual return, you'd need to have $8,100 in the account before its earnings became taxable. The second $650 of income is taxable at the child's rate, which is 15 percent, assuming she has no other income. Earnings over $1,300 a year are taxed at the parents' rate until the child turns 14. (This is the "kiddie tax" Congress imposed in 1986 to discourage use of custodial accounts as a tax shelter for parental wealth.) After the child's 14th birthday, all custodial account earnings are taxed at her rate.

There's nothing to be gained from a custodial account if you're in the same 15 percent tax bracket as your child. Its benefit is also questionable if you think your child will qualify for need-based financial aid to college.

Financial aid is designed to fill the gap between the cost of college and your family's ability to pay it. Aid formulas assume a student can pay up to 35 percent of her own assets each year for college. Parental assets, by contrast, are assessed at up to 5.65 percent.

In other words, keeping assets in your own name instead of a custodial account might let your child qualify for a bigger financial aid package.

**NOTE:** Most college aid formulas consider a stepparent's assets to be as available for tuition as those of a biological parent.

But the biggest drawback is that when you put money into a child's custodial account, you've made an irrevocable gift. You can't take it back—and as custodian, you control the money only until the child attains legal majority. In most states, that's 18—an age at which your kid may be more interested in buying a Lexus and financing a rock band than investing in a postsecondary education.

**NOTE:** The Uniform Transfer to Minors Act usually allows you to defer distributions from the custodial account until your child reaches age 21. Even if your state has adopted the Uniform Gift to Minors Act instead, you may have the option to postpone distribution of the money until the child turns 21. In New York, for example, legal majority for gifts made under the Uniform Gift to Minors Act is 18—unless you stated in writing when making the gift that it isn't to be turned over until the child is 21. To do that, all you had to do was write the words "until age 21" on the standard one-page form identifying you as the custodian, says John Dadakis, an attorney at Rogers & Wells in New York City.

What recourse do you have if that adorable baby grows into a teenager who can't handle a modest monthly allowance, let alone a six-figure college fund? Legally, none. Your child can sue you if the money isn't turned over to her.

On the other hand, few 18-year-olds seek legal advice about their rights to take possession of custodial accounts. Many parents consider it prudent to describe a custodial account as a legacy or a gift earmarked for college only—or even to let its existence slip their minds if their kid doesn't turn out as they'd hoped. "You're talking real life? I have clients whose kids are in their thirties and forties and still don't know about their custodial accounts," says one New York City tax attorney.

## Q14 What investments are appropriate or inappropriate for college?

It depends on who owns the investment and how much time you have before freshman year.

Consult your tax adviser as well as your financial planner before buying investments for your child's account. You want to avoid buying a tax-advantaged investment that loses its tax advantage when owned by a minor.

Most parents instinctively look for safety and tax breaks in a college investment. Unfortunately, investments that are promoted for safety and tax advantages also have low rates of return and high sales and management costs—a fact that isn't always mentioned by the people who sell them.

Some of these investments also charge hefty redemption fees that at best make it costly to change investments and at worst may still be in effect when you need to tap the account for the first tuition payment.

Annuities, a type of insurance contract sometimes sold as a tax-sheltered college investment, are a prime example. A fixed-income annuity guarantees you a specific rate of interest that changes every one or two years—not unlike a CD that keeps rolling over. A variable annuity lets you invest in a menu of mutual funds. In both cases, the annuity's earnings are untaxed until the money is withdrawn.

But annuities are the last thing to buy for a custodial account: any withdrawal that's taken before the annuity owner turns 59 and a half years old is subject not just to income taxes but to a 10 percent federal excise tax as well. Don't even consider an annuity as a college investment unless it's owned by a parent or grandparent who will be 59 and a half by the time the money is needed.

Even then, annuities aren't a good college investment. The redemption charge can last from five to nine years after you buy the product. Just because you're old enough to escape the government's 10 percent tax penalty doesn't necessarily mean you'll avoid the insurer's surrender penalty.

Annuities also have hefty ongoing expenses. In 1996, the average variable annuity invested in a U.S. diversified stock fund cost 2.09 percent a year, according to Morningstar; the average variable annuity invested in a fixed-income fund cost 2 percent a year. Those charges are deducted from annual returns. That's why, despite the tax-deferral, a variable annuity invested in a stock fund typically doesn't outperform a comparable taxable stock investment until you've held it for 15 years.

Cash value life insurance is also marketed as a college investment. In cash value policies, part of your premium buys insurance coverage and the rest goes into an investment account whose earnings grow untaxed until withdrawn. You can take tax-free withdrawals equal to the premiums you've paid; you can also use the policy's accumulated cash value as collateral for a loan at favorable interest.

The life insurance pitch is that when your child is ready for college, you take a policy loan to pay his tuition. In a well-structured policy, loans aren't considered taxable distributions. And agents point out that when you save in a life insurance policy, you don't reduce your child's eligibility for financial aid because under most current college aid formulas life insurance and annuities aren't considered assets available to pay tuition.

Meantime, the insurance protects the child if you die.

Here's the downside that many insurance agents don't mention: The policy's high ongoing expenses substantially reduce your return on investment. Cash value policy sales charges alone can range up to 100 percent of the first year's premium. Even if you buy a variable policy, which allows you to invest in stock funds, it typically takes 15 to 20 years to earn more in the policy than you would in a taxable investment because the policy expenses are so high.

What's more, the death benefit that's actually *guaranteed* by many variable life policies is small. Its ultimate value depends on the performance of the investments you choose. If they tank just before you're hit by a truck, the death benefit is unlikely to pay enough to cover college. Finally, college aid formulas change every year. Assets that are currently exempt may not be exempt next year—let alone a decade or more into the future. *(For more on investing for college in life insurance, see "Insurance," **Q1**.)*

Series EE bonds are worth considering for some parents. Ask your tax adviser if you meet the income test that qualifies you for a special tax exemption on the interest earned on the bonds if it is used to meet eligible college expenses.

**NOTE:** Don't put these bonds in a child's name, or you'll immediately eliminate this potential tax break. To claim the tax exemption, the bond owner must have turned 24 before the bonds were issued. (Grandparents who own EE bonds can claim the exemption only for the college tuition of grandchildren who are their dependents in the year the bonds are redeemed.)

Other pitfalls for unwary EE bond buyers: For purposes of the tax exclusion, college tuition is an eligible expense—but the cost of room, board, and books is not. And to qualify for the exemption, you must spend the money in the same year the bonds are redeemed. In other words, if you cash them in a year before your child goes to college and park the proceeds in a money market fund to earn higher interest, you blow it.

So what should you buy for a custodial account? Assuming your child won't enter college for eight years or more, you need a growth investment to beat inflation. Many financial planners recommend that you buy diversified stock funds until your child is within five years of college, and then start transferring the money into CDs or Treasuries that will mature during each of your child's college years. That investment strategy also makes sense from a tax viewpoint: Growth stock funds that focus on long-term gains won't generate much in the way of currently taxable income; most of the investment profit won't be taxable until you sell shares—after your child is 14.

Zero coupon bonds can also be a good college investment when interest rates are high, because they let you lock in the prevailing rate for the life of the bond. They're much less attractive in a low-rate environment. (You can forget about zero coupon bonds if everyone you know is thinking of refinancing his mortgage.)

A zero coupon bond is sold for a fraction of its face amount. As the name implies, you get no periodic interest payments. Instead, you receive all the interest in a lump sum along with your principal when the bond matures. Depending on current rates, you might pay as little as $300 for a Treasury zero coupon bond that returns $1,000 in 2010.

The great attraction of zeroes is their predictability: You know exactly what you'll earn, and you can buy bonds that mature in each year your child will be in college. But zeroes have two significant drawbacks: First, if you must sell them before maturity, you may take a substantial loss, since their market value fluctuates dramatically. And second, the bonds' owner (you or your child) owes taxes every year on the interest they earn, even though it isn't actually paid until the bonds mature. Interest on federal zeroes—the safest to own, since they carry no default risk—is exempt from state and local taxes. But it is federally taxable.

CHAPTER

2

# Marriage
## AND
# Divorce

MBROSE BIERCE wrote that marriage is a community consisting of a master, a mistress, and two slaves, making in all, two. That's still a pretty good definition. Marriage is also an economic partnership regulated by state and federal laws. Whether you're getting married or divorced, understanding how those laws work can save you a great deal of money.

## MARRIAGE

GETTING MARRIED IS more or less the end of financial independence for both of you—but just how much more or less is something you get to decide yourselves. There's no set formula for how married people should handle their money. You can make your own rules, and you can adapt them as your circumstances change. You can even modify your state's marital laws to suit your own circumstances if you wish by signing a prenuptial or a postnuptial contract.

Financially speaking, a successful marriage is a partnership that manages money in a way that takes maximum advantage of tax law and also satisfies both partners' idiosyncrasies. This doesn't just happen. It takes some planning—by you and your spouse and your financial advisers.

## Q1 Do I need a prenuptial agreement?

It depends on your respective finances and family obligations—and on whether you can both look at a prenuptial contract as a business matter that's totally unrelated to your feelings for one another. Don't kid yourself, though; according to people who've done it, that is as difficult as it sounds.

It's not just a figure of speech to say your spouse is your financial partner. In most states you're legally responsible for picking up the tab for each other's food, clothing, shelter, and medical care. In general, you're also liable for any debts your spouse incurs to purchase food, clothing, shelter, and medical care during your marriage.

You're automatically entitled to share each other's employee benefits. You have ownership stakes in each other's retirement accounts, survivorship rights in each other's Social Security benefits, and inheritance rights in each other's estates. Under most state laws, for example, you can't disinherit your husband or wife: Your surviving spouse typically is entitled to claim one-third of your estate, unless he or she has waived that right in a prenuptial agreement.

You may want to modify some of these entitlements with a prenuptial agreement if you have children from a previous marriage and want them to inherit the bulk of your estate, or if you've already survived one financially messy divorce and want to make sure you never experience another one.

Most prenuptial agreements really aren't about what will happen if the marriage ends in a divorce, says John Dadakis, a partner at Rogers & Wells in New York City; they're about what happens to the assets each of you brings into the marriage. The contract's main goal is to preserve your right to dispose of your prenuptial assets as you wish, rather than as state law decrees.

You may decide a prenuptial contract just isn't for you. But you and your beloved definitely should have a candid prenuptial conversation about your respective assets, debts, and attitudes towards money. It's the first step in deciding how you'll handle finances as a couple. You can create any financial system that suits you. Some couples set up a joint household account to pay all the bills. Others maintain separate accounts and divide responsibility for bills. Some couples invest separately, others invest together.

**NOTE:** If you keep separate investment portfolios, make sure you coordinate them to achieve and maintain diversification.

**NOTE:** Even if you opt for joint credit cards, keep at least one card solely in your name. If the marriage ends, this will save you the hassle of having to establish credit when you're at a financial and emotional low point.

### Q2 If we decide on a prenuptial agreement, what should it include?

It should spell out which assets you'll own jointly and which will be kept in your sole names, and how your assets will be divided in case of death or divorce.

**NOTE:** The agreement must be based on full financial disclosure, and each of you must have your own lawyer, or it won't be enforceable. Courts take a dim view of contracts in which one lawyer represented both parties, or one party concealed assets or liabilities from the other.

**NOTE:** A good agreement provides financial security to both parties. If Ralph brings $10 million to the marriage and Alice's assets are modest, she shouldn't be entitled to $5 million if the marriage ends in six months. But the longer it lasts, the more she should get if they break up. The financial provisions should include an inflation factor, too.

**NOTE:** You must be married to waive rights to each other's pensions and other employee benefits. They can't be relinquished in a prenuptial agreement.

**NOTE:** Courts do not honor prenuptial agreements regarding unborn children.

Leave yourselves plenty of time to negotiate the agreement. This contract should be settled and signed long before you're talking to wedding caterers and florists. Approach the discussions in a businesslike manner. "Love hasn't a thing to do with it," says Deena Katz, a Coral Gables, Florida, financial planner. "Take your emotional feelings about each other and put them aside."

Katz readily acknowledges that's easier said than done. She and her husband Harold Evensky, also a financial planner and her business partner, found negotiating their own prenuptial agreement "a miserable experience," she says. "We celebrated our first anniversary by sitting in the jacuzzi and burning the contract. It was our first anniversary gift to each other."

## Q3 Should we own everything jointly after we're married?

No. Joint ownership is useful, but it has some serious drawbacks.

It's financially and emotionally healthy to maintain at least a couple of individual credit cards and bank accounts. Getting married makes you partners, but it doesn't turn you and your partner into one person.

Jointly held accounts are a great convenience if one of you is incapacitated, because either of you can tap them (*see* **Q7**). Joint ownership also simplifies transfer of assets when one of you dies: The survivor automatically inherits all jointly held property without having to wait for probation of the will. That can be real plus, especially in states where probate is time-consuming and expensive.

But ask your advisers how you might be affected by the potential downside of jointly held assets:

Owning everything in joint names can result in much higher estate taxes at your deaths, if together you're worth more than $600,000. The federal tax on two $600,000 estates is nothing. The federal tax on one $1.2 million estate currently is a whopping $235,000. The government's gain is your heirs' loss. (Under the 1997 tax law, the federal estate tax exemption will gradually rise from $600,000 to $1 million over the next 10 years.)

The classic solution for a couple to avoid estate taxes on up to $1.2 million is to create a bypass trust in their wills. Each spouse leaves $600,000 to the other, and $600,000 to the trust. The trust pays lifetime income to the survivor, and, at his or her death, it passes to the couple's children. The children can inherit $600,000 from the surviving parent and $600,000 from the trust—without any estate tax due. (*For more on how to minimize estate taxes, see "Estate Planning."*)

But this neat solution won't work if the couple owns everything in joint names, because you can't dictate the disposal of jointly held property. It automatically passes to the surviving joint owner, no matter what your will says.

Joint ownership can also increase taxes on assets you sell after your spouse's death. Here's why: When spouses own property jointly, each one generally is deemed to own half, says John Dadakis, a partner at Rogers & Wells in New York City. Let's say you jointly own stock you bought for $100,000. When your spouse dies, it's worth $600,000. You inherit his half at its $300,000 market value. If you sell the stock, you'll owe a capital gains tax only on the increased value of your own half—i.e., $250,000 ($300,000 sale price minus $50,000 original cost).

But you'd inherit the stock at its full $600,000 value with no taxable gain at all if it had been held in your spouse's name alone, or if the two of you owned it as community property rather than jointly held property.

**NOTE:** If you move to a community property state—Arizona, California, Idaho, Louisiana, Nevada, New Mexico, Texas, Washington, or Wisconsin—consult a lawyer about changing from joint ownership to community ownership. (In fact, whenever you move from one state to another, it's a good idea to have a lawyer in the new state make sure that your documents conform to local law and will still give you the results you want, says Jeff Saccacio, West Coast partner in charge of personal financial services at Coopers & Lybrand in Los Angeles.)

If you don't live in a community property state, there's not much you can do about this. You could divide your assets on the basis of who's likely to die first, of course—but that won't reduce your taxes unless you guess right.

(And what if one of you is on your death bed, and you *then* transfer everything into the dying person's name? The Internal Revenue Service is way ahead of you, says Dadakis: There's an IRS rule that any asset you transfer to someone who dies within one year of the transfer doesn't get the step-up to its market value if you inherit it.)

## Q4 How should we coordinate our employee benefits?

Doing this right is an annual chore, but it can save you substantial money. Benefits are a major chunk of your compensation—often the equivalent of two or more paychecks.

Most employers now require you to pay part of the cost of your health insurance, and many charge you the full cost of dependent coverage. In exchange, you often get a wide range of choices. If you both work for big companies or municipalities, chances are that every year you both receive bulky do-it-your-self kits full of work charts, menus, and computer disks intended to help you create your own benefits package.

Bring this material to your consultation with your adviser; if you don't want to lug it all with you, each of you should at least bring your health plan's Summary Plan Document. It's also useful to bring along last year's canceled checks for the entire family's medical care. Your adviser can use them to project your likely medical expenses next year—an essential part of fig-uring out which health insurance options will work best for you.

THESE OPTIONS often include:

◆ **A traditional "indemnity" plan.** It reimburses you for 80 percent of the cost of covered medical services above an annual deductible. This is usually the most expensive option.

**NOTE:** Don't assume the indemnity plan pays 80 percent of reasonable and customary charges. Ask your employer. "Sometimes it pays only 80 percent of what your company would pay for the same services in its managed care plan," says Barry Barnett, a principal at benefits consultant Kwasha Lipton Group of Coopers & Lybrand, LLP, in Fort Lee, New Jersey.

◆ **One or more HMO plans.** In an HMO plan, you receive medical care from participating physicians, who get a predetermined annual per-patient fee. You pay no deductible, no co-insurance, and only a nomi-nal cost for office visits. The downside: you typically have no coverage outside the HMO.

◆ **One or more preferred provider organization plans**. A PPO combines features of the indemnity plan and the HMO. Participating doctors are paid on a fee-for-service basis, but they charge a discounted fee schedule. Your reimbursement is lower if you use doctors outside the PPO network.

◆ **A point-of-service plan**. This alternative is a combination of the indemnity plan and HMO. A POS lets you opt out of the HMO anytime you want and use indemnity plan coverage instead to visit a doctor who doesn't participate in the HMO, for example.

◆ **A catastrophic plan**, typically featuring very high deductibles and very high maximum annual out-of-pocket costs, but very low premiums. It's cheap—as long as you're in good health.

◆ **A flexible benefits package**. This provides a set amount of "credits" you can use to create your own plan from a menu that includes medical, dental, life, and disability insurance coverages as well as extra cash and vacation time.

AS A COUPLE, YOU HAVE two basic decisions to make: Which type of coverage to choose in each spouse's plan—indemnity, HMO, PPO, etc.—and which family members to cover in each spouse's plan. The quickest way to do this is to study the summary plan descriptions of both plans, says Barnett.

Ask your adviser to compare:

◆ **Premium cost**

◆ **Annual deductibles**—not just the amount, but whether or not you can carry deductible credit from year to year.

◆ **Co-insurance payments**—i.e., the percentage of each bill you have to pay yourself.

◆ **Out-of-pocket maximum you pay in a year**, after which you're reimbursed for 100 percent of covered expenses.

◆ **What services are covered**

◆ **How often you can change options**. If you're not satisfied with the HMO, for example, must you wait a
year to switch to the indemnity plan or the PPO?

Consider how the coverages stack up against your
actual needs, using last year's expenses as your
guide. If you have young children who see the pedi-
atrician two dozen times a year for immunization,
routine colds, and ear infections, you may prefer an
HMO. If you're being treated for a serious or
chronic condition by a doctor who isn't a member
of the HMO, you might prefer to pay more for the
indemnity plan.

**NOTE:** Ask your adviser to check the coordination of benefits clauses in both plans. It may be worthwhile to pay extra
for family coverage in both plans if you can coordinate benefits to achieve 100 percent coverage. Chances are you can't.
Increasingly, plans that pay 80 percent of covered expenses
on a primary basis also have an 80 percent limit for coordi-
nated benefits.

Some employers pay you a bonus if you decline
medical coverage altogether and you're eligible for
insurance under a spouse's plan. Ask your adviser to
estimate what you'd be giving up if you opted out of
health coverage. "You'll get about $800 to cash out of
a plan—$1,000 at most," says Barnett. "You may be
giving up $4,000 worth of benefits."

*Never* opt out of medical coverage altogether without determining that you can get it back, even if your
spouse has terrific coverage. Most plans let you back if
you've undergone a "major life event," like getting
divorced, gaining a dependent, or having a spouse
lose his or her job.

Ask your adviser's opinion of the supplementary
insurance you can buy through your employer. Typical options include:

◆ **Term life insurance without a physical examination**. If you're young and healthy, you can usually buy it less expensively outside your plan, says Barnett.

◆ **Long-term disability insurance**, which pays you a monthly stipend if you're unable to work. This is usually cheaper to buy through your employer than on your own. If you have a choice of paying for it with pretax or after-tax dollars, pay with after-tax dollars. That way, if you become disabled, your benefit will be tax free.

◆ **Dental coverage**. Ask your adviser how much is really covered under this option. "Some policies don't cover orthodontic work, others have lifetime maximums for it," says Barnett. "And sometimes the lifetime maximum is irrelevant because the policy covers so little you'll never get to the maximum anyway." Also ask how long you have to stay covered in the dental plan. Most other insurance is available annually, but many companies lock you into dental plans for two years.

◆ **Long-term care insurance** *(see "Insurance",* **Q19***).*

Don't pass up flexible spending accounts or FSAs, if your employers offer them. These accounts reduce your income taxes by letting you pay for your unreimbursed medical and child-care expenses in pretax dollars.

Your contributions to an FSA through payroll deduction are untaxed. If you're in the 31 percent tax bracket and contribute $3,000, for example, you save $930 in taxes. The catch: You must spend this money on eligible expenses before the year ends or you lose it. In other words, limit your FSA contributions to predictable expenses. Your adviser can estimate these expenses based on what you spent last year.

Annual contributions to a dependent care FSA are limited to $5,000 per household. The FSA reimburses you for day-care expenses for children under 13 and for elderly relatives. (To claim reimbursement, you must submit the caregiver's Social Security or tax ID number.)

Most companies let you set aside up to $2,000 or $3,000 in a medical FSA to pay for IRS-approved expenses that aren't covered in your health plan. Eligible expenses include your deductibles and co-payments, eyeglasses, hearing aids, orthodontic dental work, and cosmetic surgery.

## Q5 Do we need a will?

Yes. Everyone needs a will, whether married or single (see *"Estate Planning,"* **Q1**).

## Q6 Do we need a living will or a health care proxy?

Yes, if you want to preserve your right to decide what happens to you if you're incapacitated.

Don't assume anyone else has the legal right to speak for you when it comes to your medical care. In the absence of a document formally stating your wishes, these decisions will be made by the hospital and the doctors if you're unconscious—not by your nearest and dearest.

Ask your adviser which legal documents your state accepts. Most states accept either a living will or a health care proxy; some accept both. A living will specifies what medical treatment you want and don't want if you can't speak for yourself. A health care power of attorney or proxy names an agent to make your medical decisions if you're incapacitated. Both documents are revocable. You can alter them if you change your mind.

Many advisers recommend both documents, although most attorneys prefer health care proxies to living wills because they're far more flexible. (A living will must spell out every treatment you'd accept or reject, anticipating future medical treatments.)

Talk to your adviser about whom you should name as your health care proxy. This person must know what you want and also be capable of carrying out your instructions. It's a tough job. He or she must be able to talk with the doctors in a reasonably intelligent way, and also deal with other family members and friends who may want to argue with your instructions. Be sure the person you designate is willing and able to accept the job. You can make it easier by discussing your wishes ahead of time with your relatives and your doctor.

If you want to study the language of these documents before consulting an attorney, call Choice in Dying, a national nonprofit association at 800-989-WILL. It distributes living will and health care proxy forms specific to the laws of all 50 states, free of charge, with an instruction booklet explaining the peculiarities of each state law.

##  Do we need a durable power of attorney?

Yes—unless either of you could easily pay all the family's bills out of your own resources.

A will disposes of your property if you die. But what if you don't die? What if you're hit by a truck and in a coma for two weeks, or disabled for months by a stroke—who pays the bills while you're in the hospital? This isn't a problem if most of your assets are held in joint names. But without your power of attorney, your spouse won't be able to draw on any accounts that are in your sole name.

A durable power of attorney is a document in which

you give another person (or an institution) the right to act on your behalf. "Durable" means that unless you revoke it, the document will be valid until you die. A power of attorney that isn't durable expires if you become legally incompetent—which is exactly when you *want* someone else to be able to act for you.

Power of attorney forms are available at any legal stationery store. The form lists more than a dozen different powers, including the right to conduct banking transactions, the right to conduct real estate transactions, and so on. You or your lawyer can amend it to suit your own needs by adding powers that aren't listed and crossing out any power you don't want to delegate.

**NOTE:** This document gives the person you name the immediate authority to exercise every power you've granted. If that makes you even mildly uncomfortable, use a springing durable power of attorney instead: It springs into effect only under the emergency circumstances you describe in the document.

**NOTE:** Keep your springing durable power of attorney simple. You could make it effective if your regular attending physician or two other doctors agree that you're incapacitated, for example. If the document's emergency conditions are so detailed that your spouse has to go to court to prove they've been met, you've defeated your objective.

**NOTE:** A more complicated alternative to the power of attorney is a living trust (*see "Estate Planning,"* **Q6**).

## DIVORCE

FINANCIALLY SPEAKING, a successful divorce is one that preserves your accumulated marital assets to the greatest possible extent and splits them fairly between you.

That doesn't happen unless you can both approach

the dissolution of your partnership with a modicum of equity and common sense. A good financial adviser can make that much likelier by showing you how cooperation will minimize the financial damage to both parties.

## Q8 What should be my financial priorities in a divorce?

Predivorce planning may be the most important financial planning you ever do. It can result in a settlement that's fairer to both of you, and much less expensive because it's achieved more quickly, minimizing legal fees.

You need to understand the big picture *before* you sit down to negotiate a divorce settlement. Ask your lawyer to explain your rights and options under state law. Ask your financial planner and/or tax accountant to help you inventory your marital assets and liabilities, and explain how the dissolution of your marriage will affect your personal finances.

Your financial advisers will need to see copies of your tax returns for the past several years (available from the IRS, if you don't have them); your bank, brokerage, and mutual fund statements; your insurance policies; all employment-related financial data, including your paycheck stubs and retirement plan statements; the deed to the house and to any other property you own; and your credit histories. You're both responsible for many of the debts incurred during your marriage.

If your assets include limited partnerships, real estate, or closely held family businesses, they should be independently appraised by someone qualified to do the job.

Your immediate priorities include:

◆ Opening a new checking account in your name alone and applying for your own credit card, if you don't already have them.

◆ Notifying your broker that from now on, both of you must approve any transactions in your jointly held brokerage accounts. Normally, securities held in a joint account can be sold or transferred by either owner without the other one's signature.

◆ Notifying the bank to freeze your jointly held savings and checking accounts and your home equity line of credit.

◆ Notifying credit card companies that you will no longer be responsible for the charges on any joint credit cards.

You should do all this in writing and send the letters return receipt requested. You should also revoke any power of attorney you've given your spouse.

Division of marital assets depends on state law. If you live in a community property state, you're each entitled to 50 percent of marital assets. If you live in an equitable distribution state, each of you is entitled to a fair share of the assets accumulated during your marriage, no matter whose name they're in. What's a fair share is subject to negotiation, which is one reason people hire divorce lawyers. The ultimate decision is made by the divorce court.

Your divorce settlement should address your future needs as well as your current ones. The parent who provides child support should be covered by life insurance, for example, to replace those payments in the event of his or her death. The settlement should address new expenses, such as additional child-care expenses that will be incurred as a result of the divorce.

If you're a woman who left the work-force during your marriage, ask your adviser to make sure the settlement will:

**1** Enhance your ability to get a good job;

**2** Preserve your health insurance; *and*
**3** Preserve your right to retirement income from your spouse's pension.

The only way to achieve financial independence after divorce is to earn a living wage. That's why you should make it a priority to get temporary maintenance that will give you time to improve your job skills and return to work with reasonable earning power, says Larry Elkin, a financial planner in Hastings-on-Hudson, New York.

You're legally entitled to be your spouse's designated beneficiary in all private sector qualified retirement plans, unless you sign a consent waiver surrendering the right. You should avoid doing that if you have no retirement plan of your own.

Retirement assets in either spouse's name that accumulated during the marriage are considered a marital asset. This includes IRAs, Keogh accounts, profit-sharing plans, 401(k) plans, stock-option plans, and pensions. If you were married for two years and in your employer's retirement plan for three years, for example, two-thirds of that pension would be considered a marital asset.

You won't receive payments from your spouse's defined benefit pension until he or she reaches retirement age. But you can receive your share of his or her 401(k) or other defined contribution plan when you get divorced. If you don't roll this money into an IRA, you'll owe taxes on it. But you'll escape the additional 10 percent early withdrawal penalty normally levied if you're under age 59 and a half.

**NOTE:** Ask your lawyer to get a court order—it's called a Qualified Domestic Relations Order—instructing the administrator of your spouse's retirement plan to segregate your share of his or her account. Your lawyer should do this even if your spouse participates in a public sector pension. Public retirement plans aren't covered by the federal law that protects spouses in private pensions; but matrimonial lawyers say that in practice, they, too, respond to this type of court order.

If your marriage lasted at least 10 years and you haven't remarried, you qualify for a Social Security benefit based on your former spouse's earnings.

**NOTE:** If you're just a few months shy of the 10 years and have no retirement plan of your own, consider delaying the divorce. You'll get the spousal benefit or a Social Security benefit based on your own earnings, whichever is larger—not both. (For more information on how changes in your marital status can affect your Social Security benefits, call the Social Security Administration at 800-772-1213.)

If your spouse's company employs at least 20 people, you're automatically entitled to receive health insurance from its employee benefits plan for 36 months after your divorce is final. You must request the coverage in writing. This coverage gives you the advantage of a discounted group premium, which is usually much less than you'd pay as an individual policyholder. But your premium won't be subsidized by your ex-spouse's employer. You must pay the full amount, plus a 2 percent administrative fee. That can be very expensive, so it's another issue you may want your lawyer to address in the divorce settlement.

**NOTE:** Your divorce settlement can stipulate that you and/or your children must receive continued health coverage under your former spouse's group health plan. Employers must respect a certified court order to that effect, says Barry Barnett, a principal at benefits consultant Kwasha Lipton Group of Coopers & Lybrand LLP. (The employer can charge your ex-spouse for this dependent coverage, of course.)

## Q9 How can we minimize the cost of the divorce? Are there pitfalls to avoid?

Focus on getting a decent financial settlement, not on getting even—and don't sign anything before finding out the tax consequences.

You and your spouse and children aren't the only parties to your divorce. The Internal Revenue Service has a major role, too. Pay attention to how the *after-tax* proceeds are divided between you.

A $150,000 stock portfolio and a $150,000 house have the same fair market value, for example, but they may have very different tax liabilities. Let's say the stock was originally bought for $75,000 and the house for $50,000. When the two assets are sold, the spouse who gets the stock will owe taxes on a $75,000 capital gain, but the one who gets the house will have a $100,000 profit that is tax-free under the 1997 tax law: The new law exempts the first $500,000 of profit on the sale of a principal residence by a married couple filing jointly, and the first $250,000 of profit for an individual taxpayer.

The tax consequences of divorce can be particularly unfair when it comes to a house, often a couple's biggest single asset. When a marriage breaks up, one partner often stays in the house and the other moves out. Sometimes the spouse who leaves transfers title to the house to the one who stays; they agree that when the house is eventually sold, they'll split the proceeds.

This is a bad deal for the one who gets title to the house if it turns out there's a taxable capital gain when it is sold, says Alan Weiner, senior tax partner at Holtz Rubenstein in Melville, New York. Here's why:

If there is a tax, the person who got title to the house will owe the entire amount, while the other spouse gets his or her half of the proceeds tax-free.

"Let's say that house originally cost $150,000," says Weiner. "You have title to the house now and you sell it for $500,000 and give your ex-husband $250,000. As the sole owner, you have a $350,000 profit—the $500,000 sale price minus the $150,000 original cost. The IRS doesn't give you credit for the $250,000 you gave him."

Your ex-spouse doesn't owe taxes on that $250,000, because it's considered a 'property transfer incident to divorce', which isn't taxable. But as a single taxpayer, you owe a capital gains tax on any profit in excess of $250,000—in this example, $100,000.

Ask your attorney to make sure that any extra tax burdens on either spouse be factored into the total property settlement. One way to do that is to give him or her a larger share of another asset.

**NOTE:** If you sign away your share of the house, try to get your name off the mortgage. The mortgage lender isn't a party to your separation agreement any more than the IRS. If your name is on the loan, the lender can and will come after you if your former spouse is unable to make the payments. When two people borrow, each is responsible for the full amount of the loan. (Besides, as long as your name is on this mortgage, you're unlikely to qualify for another one.)

Both spouses come out ahead financially when they cooperate. One divorce lawyer's favorite example: A husband pays mortgage and property taxes directly to the bank as part of a divorce settlement, but he's no longer on the deed. He's not entitled to a tax deduction because he doesn't own the house. But alimony is deductible to him. A better arrangement is for the husband to pay alimony equal to the mortgage payment to his wife. Then she can pay the mortgage and deduct it—and he can deduct the alimony. (But the alimony will be taxable income to her.)

**NOTE:** One way you can save money is to hire a mediator instead of two divorce lawyers. A mediator isn't an advocate; his interest is simply in achieving an agreement. Bear in mind, however, that a mediator's priority isn't necessarily a fair agreement. If your spouse has a forceful personality and you're a pushover, you'd probably do better with a lawyer fighting for you than you will in mediation.

**NOTE:** If you opt for a lawyer, don't run up the bill by crying on his or her shoulder. Lawyers charge higher hourly rates than therapists.

## Q10 If we sell the house and split the profits, should we sell it before or after the divorce?

This longstanding dilemma has been eased by the new tax act that President Clinton signed into law on August 5, 1997. But the real impact of a new tax law usually doesn't become clear until many months after it's enacted. You should discuss your specific situation with your tax adviser.

The 1997 law grants a tax exclusion on profits from the sale of a primary residence up to $500,000 for a married couple filing jointly, and up to $250,000 for single taxpayers.

This new rule replaces two old ones: The tax exclusion on profits that were rolled into the purchase of a new primary residence within two years, and the one-time exclusion on profits up to $125,000 for people 55 years old or older who sold a house they'd lived in for three of the previous five years both have been eliminated.

The $500,000/$250,000 tax exclusion is available only if the house you sell is your principal residence, which the new law defines as a house you have owned and lived in for two of the past five years. In a divorce situation, one spouse often has moved out before the house is sold, notes Alan Weiner, but as long as that person can show he lived there for two of the five years before the sale, his share of the profit should qualify for the tax exclusion.

A potential snag is that if you have young children, the delay in selling the house after the divorce could be too long to let the spouse who moved out claim the exclusion. Courts typically grant the custodial parent exclusive occupancy of the house until the youngest child is 18, because it's extremely disruptive for kids to be forced to leave their home.

If the spouse who moved out (typically the husband) but kept title to the house can no longer claim it as his primary residence when it's sold, his share of the profit will be subject to long-term capital gains tax, which under the new law is now capped at 20 percent. If you face this situation, you should ask your legal and tax advisers to make sure that any adverse tax consequences to the person who moves out are factored into the total divorce settlement.

CHAPTER

3

OR MOST PEOPLE, a house is the biggest single investment and the biggest tax break—and for most people, that break became even better this year. The 1997 tax law excludes up to $500,000 of profit on the sale of a primary residence for married couples filing jointly, and up to $250,000 for single taxpayers. You must have owned and lived in the house for at least two of the past five years to claim this exclusion.

Your house is really the original life-cycle investment: You can borrow against it to send the kids to college, repay the home equity loan out of your retirement accounts after you turn 59 and a half, and then sell the house to buy a retirement cottage.

That's the upside.

The downside is that houses eat money. Routine maintenance and major repairs and property taxes and insurance always add up to more than you expected.

## Q1 How much can I borrow to buy a house?

It depends on your income, on how much debt you already have, and on current interest rates.

For mortgages up to $214,600, the lender's rule-of-thumb is that your total monthly housing cost—mortgage payment, property taxes, and homeowners insurance—should total no more than 28 percent of your monthly gross income. Your monthly payments on all outstanding debt—housing costs, alimony and child support obligations, student loans, credit card debt, and any installment debt on which there are 10 payments or more to go—generally can't exceed

36 percent of your monthly gross income.

Lenders are a bit more generous if you're borrowing more than $214,600; your monthly housing cost and total debt payments can add up to 33 percent and 38 percent of your income, respectively. Sometimes they'll stretch the debt-to-income ratio even more if your credit is good. And most banks will give you more leeway than usual on your debt payments if you're a doctor or a lawyer with huge student loans, says Jeffrey Tuchman, president of The Mortgage Shopper, a Pleasantville, New York, company that finds mortgages for borrowers for a flat fee.

You can quickly estimate how much you can borrow on a pocket calculator. All you need is the total amount of your outstanding monthly debt payments and a copy of *Barron's Financial Guide to Mortgage Payments,* a small, dark-blue paperback available at any bookstore or library. The book gives the monthly cost of mortgage loans at different terms and interest rates. At 8.5 percent interest, a 30-year $100,000 loan costs $768.91 a month, for example. At 6.5 percent interest, the same loan would cost $632.07 a month; at 9 percent interest, it would cost $804.62 a month.

Let's assume you earn $60,000 a year and pay $500 a month to creditors. Divide your gross annual income by 12 to get your monthly income—$5,000. Multiply that monthly income by 36 percent to find out the maximum monthly debt you're allowed under bank guidelines—$1,800. Subtract your current monthly debt ($1,800 minus $500) and the result is the maximum housing cost a bank will think you can afford: $1,300 a month for mortgage, homeowners insurance, and property taxes.

But that doesn't mean you really can afford it.

On paper, you're likely to qualify for a bigger mortgage than you can comfortably carry, because the lender's debt guidelines don't factor in monthly expenditures like the cost of child care, medical care, life insurance, or investing for retirement, let alone expenses like eating out, going to the movies, or taking an annual vacation.

You also need cash in hand for a downpayment, which is generally equal to 20 percent of the purchase price.

**NOTE:** This downpayment doesn't include closing costs—miscellaneous fees that themselves can total up to 7 percent of the purchase price in some parts of the country.

But your downpayment can be as little as 5 percent of the purchase price, if your credit is good. Most lenders want that 5 percent downpayment to be your own money, not a gift from your parents, says Tuchman. (A loan from your 401(k) plan qualifies as your own money; but your repayments to the 401(k) plan are included in the debt-to-income calculation. There are also risks to borrowing from your 401(k) plan (*see "Losing Your Job"*).)

If your downpayment is only 5 percent, you usually must agree to buy private mortgage insurance. PMI isn't the same as the insurance you buy so your family can pay off the mortgage if you die. PMI protects only the bank—it pays off your loan if you default. The premiums are added to your monthly mortgage payments.

**NOTE:** You're required to carry PMI only as long as your stake in the house is less than 20 percent of its value. Some lenders don't bother to notify you when that happens. If you pay for PMI, be sure to cancel it when your annual mortgage statement shows that your outstanding principal on the loan has dropped to 80 percent or less of the price you paid for the house.

**NOTE:** Ask the loan officer if there are alternatives to PMI. "Some lenders will charge you about a quarter of a percentage point higher interest on the loan instead," says Tuchman. "That works out slightly better than PMI for you over the long haul because, generally, all the interest on the mortgage is tax-deductible."

## Q2 How much should I plan to spend?

Don't stretch to buy the most expensive house you can. This will probably be your biggest single investment—but if it's too big an investment, it can distort your personal finances for years to come.

In deciding how big an expenditure makes sense for you, you and your financial planner or tax accountant should discuss the following: your current income and expenses and expected future increases in your income; any big predictable future expenses (such as tuition bills); your future career plans (do you expect or hope to move within the next few years?); and your investment portfolio. What other assets do you own? Will you have enough disposable income to keep adding to them after buying a house?

Consider a couple who together earn $65,000, but have $250,000 in combined savings and inherited assets. Theoretically, they can afford to put down $200,000 for a $300,000 house and pay $7,000 a year in property taxes. The taxes plus a 30-year $100,000 mortgage at 8.5 percent interest will cost $15,500 a year. That's only about a quarter of their income.

But in real life, the cost of utilities, maintenance, yard work, and furnishings for a $300,000 house may bring the actual tab closer to $25,000 a year even if the property taxes don't go up, which, of course, they will. Instead of feeling carefree because of their big inheritance, this couple may wind up feeling strapped for cash.

Also, they will have invested the lion's share of their

assets in their house—an illiquid, undiversified, and highly leveraged investment.

(Here's how leverage works: You buy a $100,000 house with just $20,000—a 20 percent downpayment. Its value increases 20 percent, to $120,000. That 20 percent increase represents a 100 percent increase in the value of your $20,000 stake. That's the best-case scenario. The worst case: the house loses 20 percent of its value and your $20,000 stake is wiped out. If its value falls even more, you can wind up with a mortgage bigger than the market value of the house.)

This couple would do much better looking for a house in the $150,000 to $175,000 range in a neighborhood where the biggest houses sell for twice as much, and investing their inheritance elsewhere, says Ray Russolillo, director of personal financial services at Price Waterhouse in New York City.

Real estate prices tend to keep pace with inflation. The World War II generation had a windfall in their houses, thanks to the soaring inflation of the 1970s and 1980s. But inflation is much more modest in the 1990s. Also, baby-boom homeowners outnumber the demographic group that follows them, which means the supply of houses for sale may outstrip future demand. The bottom line: the value of houses is likely to grow much more modestly than in the past.

**Q3** **If I get my mortgage from a member of my family, what should we do to make sure it's a legitimate mortgage for tax purposes?**

Make it a business deal that any prudent person would do with a nonrelative. Pretend the prudent person in question works for the IRS.

Ask your tax adviser what interest rate and terms would be appropriate for an intrafamily loan. A mortgage from a family member can be a more generous deal than you'd get from a bank—but if it's too generous, the IRS will conclude that the money is a gift rather than a loan. Aunt Mary doesn't have to charge you points or service fees on her loan, but she must charge more than a nominal rate of interest—and she can't lend you more than the house is worth.

Ideally, Aunt Mary gets a higher interest rate on her note, and you get a lower interest rate on your mortgage, than either one of you would from a bank.

The potential snag is that you may not treat it as a business deal. Maybe you'll be less conscientious about making payments than if you'd borrowed from a bank. Maybe your aunt will be reluctant to foreclose on you even if you're not making your payments. Maybe even if you make every payment on time, she'll feel her loan entitles her to comment extensively on your personal or professional decisions.

**NOTE:** Record the mortgage with the county clerk or city registrar. If the mortgage isn't recorded, the borrower isn't entitled to an income tax deduction for the interest she pays on it, says Alan Weiner, senior tax partner at Holtz Rubenstein in Melville, New York. "It's also a good idea for both parties to list their names, addresses, and Social Security numbers in reporting the mortgage interest on their income tax returns," he adds.

Recording the mortgage is important from the lender's viewpoint, too, because it establishes his or her interest in the house, says Theodore Harris, a New York tax lawyer. That way, if the borrower winds up in bankruptcy court, the house can't be sold to satisfy other debts unless the mortgage is paid off first.

A recorded mortgage also minimizes nasty disagreements if family relationships change down the road: "There are parents who are happy to make their child a loan, but who worry about the child's spouse," says Harris. "They envision a divorce in which their child's spouse gets the house and says 'What loan? That was a gift.' When the mortgage has been recorded, there's no argument about whether it was a gift or a loan."

## Q4 What kind of mortgage makes sense for me?

It depends on how much you need to borrow and how long you're likely to own the house. Ask your financial planner or tax accountant to crunch the numbers for you.

The granddaddy of all mortgages is a 30-year fixed-rate loan. You pay a higher interest rate on a fixed-rate mortgage than on an adjustable-rate mortgage (ARM), but you have the security of a totally pre-dictable monthly cost. Fixed-rate mortgages typically are available for 10-, 15-, or 30-year terms. The longer the term, the smaller your monthly payments, but the greater the total amount of interest you'll pay over the life of the loan.

An ARM has a lower initial interest rate, which means you can borrow more; but your interest rate and your monthly mortgage payment will move up and down in line with a short-term index, like the rate on one-year Treasury bills, for example. With an ARM, you benefit from any drop in interest rates without having to refinance your mortgage. But you're also exposed to any increase in rates.

In general, an ARM is attractive for buyers who expect to own a house for only a few years. The longer you plan to stay in the house, the greater your exposure to interest rate risk and the better off you are with a fixed mortgage—especially if you can lock in a low rate.

"If you can lock in a fixed rate below 8 percent for 15 or 30 years, it makes little sense to take an adjustable-rate mortgage unless you know you're going to be moving in a certain amount of time," says

Jeffrey Tuchman, a Pleasantville, New York, mortgage consultant. "But if fixed-rate mortgages are above 8 percent, you're almost certain to get the chance to refinance your mortgage at a lower rate down the road. So why not save money until then by taking an adjustable-rate mortgage?"

The beauty of ARMs is that they offer a combination of fixed and adjustable rates. A 10-year ARM, for example, in reality is a fixed-rate loan for the first 10 years and is then adjusted annually for the next 20 years. "A 10-year ARM should cost half a percentage point less than the rate on 30-year fixed mortgages," says Tuchman. In other words, if you know you'll be moving in 10 years, a 10-year ARM is a good way to get a lower fixed-rate mortgage.

ARMs come in a wide variety of terms, including seven-, five-, three-, and one-year periods.

Comparison shopping is essential. There are six basic questions to ask mortgage lenders once you've decided an ARM is for you:

**1 How often does the rate change after the mortgage becomes adjustable?** This matters if you plan to keep the mortgage beyond the initial fixed term. Typically, the ARM rate changes annually, but the adjustment period can range from six months to several years. A three-year ARM is widely available in two flavors, for example. One has a fixed rate for three years and then is adjusted annually; the other is fixed for three years and is then adjusted every three years.

**2 What's the benchmark used to set the rate?** The one-year Treasury bill is a common benchmark, for example. An ARM that has a fixed rate for three years and then is adjusted every three years usually is pegged to the three-year Treasury, says Tuchman.

**3 What's the margin, i.e., the number of points that are added to the benchmark to determine your interest rate?** The typical margin is 2 or 3 percent. If the benchmark is 5 percent and the margin is 3 percent, your interest rate will be 8 percent.

**4** What's the ARM cap, i.e., the most your rate can rise or fall with each adjustment? Typically, ARMs have a 2 percent one-year cap and a 6 percent lifetime cap.

**NOTE:** Don't take an ARM without calculating the highest possible monthly payment, assuming you had to pay the lifetime cap. If that maximum payment would wipe you out, you can't afford the loan.

**NOTE:** Also ask what the cap is for the first adjustment on the ARM. "Avoid banks that will let the first ARM adjustment go up to the lifetime cap," says Tuchman.

**5** How long does the introductory interest rate last? Some lenders offer very low teaser rates. If you know what it is, at least you won't be taken by surprise when the introduction is over.

**6** Is negative amortization possible with this loan? Some ARMs are sold with the assurance that your monthly payments can never go above a stated amount, no matter what happens to interest rates. That sounds great, but there's a huge potential cost: If your capped monthly payments are too low to cover the interest required to pay off the loan, whatever you should have paid but didn't is added to the original loan. "Let's say that because rates have gone up, your payments should be $1,500 a month to amortize the loan in 30 years, but your payment is capped at $1,200," says Tuchman. "The $300 a month you're not paying is added to your mortgage balance."

The result: Instead of reducing your outstanding mortgage, your monthly payments actually increase it.

Your mortgage interest is the price of the loan—but it may not be the only price. You may also pay 'points'—an additional upfront payment in return for which you get a lower interest rate. One point is equal to 1 percent of the loan amount. Two points on a

$100,000 mortgage would be $2,000, for example. On a fixed-rate mortgage, the more points you pay, the lower the interest rate for the life of the loan. On an ARM, points can lower the lifetime cap on your loan as well as the initial rate.

"Each point you pay typically lowers your interest by a quarter percentage point," says Tuchman. "That's the standard 'buy-down.'" But be on the lookout for bargains. Sometimes, paying one point will cut your interest rate by as much as three-eighths or half a percentage point. "That means the loan is on sale," says Tuchman. "It's priced so that the savings you'll get every month from the lower interest rate will offset the points you pay at closing more quickly than the usual time, which is five years."

Tuchman advises against paying points if you'll own the house for only five years or less, or if interest rates are above 8 percent, making it likely that you'll be able to refinance at a lower rate within five years.

## Q5  Which closing costs are tax-deductible?

Too few.

Closing costs are the bill for services you can't refuse if you want a mortgage. They vary from one lender to another, but they're not insignificant: they can add up to 7 percent of the amount of the loan. In other words, a $100,000 mortgage could entail as much as $7,000 in closing costs.

Closing costs can include:

◆ **Loan application and processing fees**. Would you believe that even after you and your spouse have filled out multiple-page application forms and gathered and photocopied and given the bank two years' worth of your income tax returns, bank statements, retirement account statements, and other financial documents, there's still paperwork left to be done by bank personnel? This is the bill for that paperwork.

◆ **Fee for the credit reports** that the bank buys to find out if you're creditworthy.

◆ **Fee for title search and title insurance** showing that the seller really is entitled to sell the house. The bank requires title insurance to protect itself against the risk that after you pay for your house, it will turn out that the seller didn't really own it. The policy protects you against that risk, too.

◆ **Fee for a survey to show the exact boundaries** of the property you're buying. This is what you'll whip out years from now to make your neighbor back down from trying to build his gazebo on your land.

◆ **Underwriting fee.** It pays for the bank's appraisal to make sure the house is worth enough to cover the loan if you default. (*Note:* You will pay separately for your own (much more thorough) inspection of the house to check the condition of its electrical, heating, and plumbing systems, not to mention the foundation and the roof, etc.)

◆ **Loan points, sometimes called an origination fee**, to reduce the interest rate charged on the mortgage (*see pages **75** and **76***).

◆ **Lawyers' fees.** The bank always has a lawyer. In some parts of the country, it's customary for you to have a lawyer, too; in others, it isn't. In any event, you pay your lawyer *and* the bank's lawyer.

◆ **Escrow account deposit.** This is your check for several months' worth of future property taxes and homeowners insurance premiums. The bank keeps your money and pays these taxes and premiums for you as they fall due.

**NOTE:** You can reduce the cash drain at your closing by opting to be responsible for paying these bills yourself, if the bank doesn't require an escrow account.

◆ Fee for filing the deed.
◆ Fee for recording the mortgage.
◆ Mortgage tax.

So what can you deduct?

On a new mortgage, any points you pay are tax-deductible in the year you pay them. (Even if you add the points to the loan, they're deductible in the year you buy the house, if the points are less than your down payment.) If you're refinancing an existing mortgage, points are deductible only over the life of the new mortgage.

**NOTE:** "Points are tax-deductible to the buyer even if the seller pays them," says Ed Slott, a Rockville Centre, New York, tax accountant and author of *Your Tax Questions Answered.*

Any amount you pay to reimburse the seller for local taxes that he or she has already paid on the property is fully tax-deductible. Amounts in the escrow account to cover property taxes are deductible only as they are paid out. Homeowners insurance premiums aren't deductible.

There's no tax deduction for loan application or processing fees, credit report fees, or the cost of private mortgage insurance *(see* **Q1***)*. Nor can you deduct the cost of the title search and title insurance, property survey, underwriting fee, attorneys' fees, mortgage tax, or filing fees—but all those expenses do count as part of the total cost of the house.

Those costs will reduce your taxes on any profit you make when you sell the house because the greater your original cost, the smaller your gain when you sell. You can add any real estate agents' commissions to the cost of the house, too.

## Q6 Should I buy mortgage life insurance?

Only if you're ineligible for regular term life insurance, which is very unlikely.

Mortgage life insurance costs more than a regular term policy, and it only covers one expense—the mortgage. Your survivors don't have the option of using the policy proceeds for anything else. Instead, buy a regular policy in an amount large enough to cover the mortgage along with your survivors' other expenses.

## Q7 How should we own the house, jointly or in separate names?

It depends partly on your marital status and partly on how rich you are. Married couples with more than $600,000 in assets can substantially reduce their estate taxes by splitting ownership of their assets between them (see "Marriage and Divorce," **Q3**, and "Estate Planning," **Q7** and **Q8**.)

There are basically three ways to own a house together: jointly with right of survivorship, jointly by the entirety, or as tenants-in-common. You don't have to be married to own jointly with right of survivorship or as tenants-in-common, but joint ownership by the entirety is available only to married couples (and not in all states).

When you own a house jointly with right of survivorship, neither of you can sell the property without the other's consent. Both your signatures are necessary on all transactions. Neither of you can dispose of the house by will: When one partner dies, the survivor automatically inherits the entire property.

**NOTE:** But if one of you is in debt, that person's creditors can go to court and force a sale of the house in order to recover their money from his or her share of the proceeds.

When a married couple owns a house jointly by the entirety, it's exempt from either spouse's creditors. "Let's say the husband is in debt. His creditors can sue and get a lien on the property—but they can't force a sale," says Alan Weiner, senior tax partner at Holtz Rubenstein in Melville, New York. "If the wife dies first, then the husband owns 100 percent of the property, and his creditors can force a sale to collect. But if the husband dies first, his creditors are out in the cold. The wife owns the entire property and the husband's creditors never get their money back."

In nine states (Arizona, California, Idaho, Louisiana, Nevada, New Mexico, Texas, Washington, and Wisconsin), married couples can own their house as community property. An owner of community property can leave his or her share by will to anyone he or she chooses.

**NOTE:** There's also an income tax advantage to owning community property: One owner can inherit property from the other at its full fair market value and sell it without owing taxes on the profit (*see "Marriage and Divorce,"* **Q3**).

Friends and siblings usually are better off owning as tenants-in-common. That allows them to sell or leave their respective interests separately, to anyone they wish. (*Note:* If a married couple divorce, in some states they automatically become tenants-in-common, regardless of how they owned the property before.)

Of course, a sale by one tenant-in-common could land the other one with a new co-owner he doesn't like. If you're planning to own a house as tenants-in-common, ask your lawyer or financial planner to draw up a simple agreement that gives each of you first right of refusal on any sale. "It's also a good idea to keep a record of what each of you has paid in mortgage, property taxes, and maintenance—or you'll have trouble figuring out your respective total investments in the property when it's time to sell," says Ed Slott.

Each tenant-in-common can take income tax deductions only for amounts he or she has actually paid—but if you cosigned the mortgage, each of you is on the hook for 100 percent of the loan as far as the bank's concerned, no matter who signs the checks.

**NOTE:** The form of ownership you choose affects your estate taxes when you die. When a married couple owns a house jointly, each spouse is presumed to own 50 percent of its value for tax purposes. As a result, when one spouse dies, only half the value of the house is included in his or her estate. A $300,000 house would be valued at $150,000, for example.

But that's only true if the joint owners are married. When nonspouses own property in joint names, the IRS assumes the first one to die owned the entire property, and its full value is included in his or her taxable estate. The survivor can refute that assumption by showing that he or she contributed to the purchase. (*Note*: If you own jointly and aren't married, keep good records. The IRS will want more than your word for what you invested in the house.)

## Q8 What records should I keep of home repairs and/or improvements?

The 1997 tax law has made it much less important for most people to keep careful records of the money they spend on capital improvements to a primary residence.

Any money you spent on capital improvements over the years reduces your taxable profit when you sell your house. Under the 1997 law, however, your profit isn't taxable unless it exceeds $500,000 for married couples filing jointly, or $250,000 for single taxpayers. (To qualify for the exclusion, you must have owned and lived in the house for two of the past five years.)

But keeping records still matters if you have reason to think your profit on the sale of the house will exceed $500,000 (or $250,000, if you're single), if you're selling a vacation house or rental property, or if you're a divorced person who's no longer eligible to claim the house in question as his or her primary residence.

You don't have to attach receipts for these expenses to your tax return when you report your profit from the sale—but you'll need them if you're audited and the IRS asks you to back up whatever amount you claimed for capital improvements.

IRS guidelines say that to qualify as a capital improvement, your expenditure must "materially add value to the property, prolong its life, or make it adaptable to a different use." This would include the cost of finishing a basement, for example, or replacing a roof, adding a bathroom, putting in new wiring or plumbing, or paving your driveway.

The cost of repairs and routine maintenance—expenses that merely keep your house in working order—doesn't count as a capital improvement. Neither does the cost of making your house more livable by replacing hideous wallpaper and crumbling kitchen linoleum. As far as the IRS is concerned, those changes don't materially add to the value of the house. "Think of repairs as replacing value, not adding it," advises tax accountant Ed Slott. "Replacing broken window panes is a repair. Putting in new windows is a capital improvement."

When you sell your vacation house, you'll add the cost of capital improvements to the price you originally paid for the house. Let's say you originally paid $100,000 for it, and you spent $50,000 on improvements. So your total cost was $150,000. You sell the house for $230,000. Your taxable profit is $230,000 minus $150,000—$80,000. (IRS publications that explain how to calculate tax treatment of your profit on the sale of a house are 523, *Selling Your Home* and 551, *Basis of Assets.* You can order them free of charge by calling the IRS at 800-829-3676.)

**NOTE:** Don't panic if you haven't saved all those receipts and canceled checks for repairs and improvements. The IRS will accept a reasonable estimate, especially if you have before and after pictures. "If you've owned a house for 30 years, chances are you've invested tens of thousands of dollars in improvements," says Slott. "Walk slowly through the house, remembering what it was originally like. Go through old photo albums. List the major changes and estimate the cost, based on when the work was done."

## Q9 Does it makes sense to prepay my mortgage or should I use the money to invest elsewhere?

That depends on the cost of the mortgage, your appetite for risk, and your age.

People often assume it's a mistake to pay off a mortgage, because it represents a tax deduction. But tax deductions don't put money into your pocket; they just reduce your expenses. If you're in a 33 percent combined federal and state income bracket, $100 of mortgage interest costs you only $67 after taxes—but that's $67 that you'd save if you paid off the mortgage.

Prepaying the mortgage doesn't reduce your monthly payment, but it may be worthwhile because it shortens the term of the loan, saving you thousands of dollars of interest. "As a general rule, on a 30-year mortgage, you save $3 for approximately every $1 prepaid," says Jeffrey Tuchman, a mortgage consultant. "On an after-tax basis, you get back $2 for every $1 you prepay."

Paying down the mortgage is a risk-free investment, and it can be done with extremely small sums of money. A simple method is to round your monthly payment up to the nearest $100. If you're paying $783.20 a month, for example, write the check for $800. You know exactly what you'll earn on that additional $16.80 a month: if your mortgage costs 8 percent a year in interest, 8 percent is your rate of return on prepayment.

To decide if prepaying the mortgage is the best use of your money, ask your financial planner how that return stacks up against what you'd earn in other investments. Could you earn more by investing in a comparably safe investment, like a CD or Treasury bill, for example?

**NOTE:** Only consider alternative investments that you'd really make. Sure, over periods of a decade or more, you can expect to earn 10 percent a year in the stock market. But stocks are a riskier investment than prepaying a mortgage— and your potential return in stocks is irrelevant in any case, if CDs are the only investment you'd seriously consider.

**NOTE:** The first alternative investment to consider is paying off your credit card debt. If your credit card balance costs you 18 percent interest a year, don't even *think* about prepaying an 8 percent mortgage instead.

**NOTE:** Don't prepay the mortgage if your house is your sole asset. A house is an illiquid, undiversified investment. Diversify by investing your available cash elsewhere.

Other factors to discuss with your financial planner:

◆ **Your time horizon.** Prepaying the mortgage makes sense if you're nearing retirement, have other investments, and want to reduce your living expenses. But if your retirement is more than a decade away, stock mutual funds are a much more diversified investment than your house and pay a higher return—especially if you can buy them through a tax-deferred retirement account.

◆ **Your cash flow.** You don't want to wind up strapped for money because it's all in the house. If you lost your job or suffered a serious illness, how quickly could you tap the house for cash? Would you qualify for a home equity loan under those circumstances—and what would it cost?

Before prepaying, make sure your bank won't charge you a penalty. Also make sure the bank gives you appropriate credit for the amounts you prepay. "Most banks are set up to take monthly prepayments," says Tuchman. "But others don't know what to do with the extra money. They throw it into another account—an interest-bearing account, for example, or an escrow account for real estate taxes. Include a short note with your check asking the bank to apply the extra amount to the mortgage principal."

**NOTE:** Some lenders offer to sell you a biweekly mortgage conversion plan that lets you make one extra monthly mortgage payment over the course of a year. Don't buy it. The same lenders will let you prepay for free by adding any amount you wish to your regular monthly payment.

## Q10 Should I consider establishing a home equity line of credit?

Yes. But try not to use it.

A home equity line of credit can be a cheap insurance policy if you plan to retire early or fear you may lose your job. But as with all insurance policies, you're better off if you don't have to use it. In general, your home equity is last-resort money, like your retirement accounts.

The traditional second mortgage is a fixed amount that you borrow at a fixed interest rate, for a fixed term—$10,000 at 9 percent interest for 10 years, for example. A home equity line of credit is an open-ended second mortgage with a variable interest rate. In either case, the interest is tax deductible on loans up to $100,000 because your house is the collateral.

A home equity line works somewhat like a credit card. You're approved to borrow a maximum amount of money, which you can draw on as you need it by writing checks. The credit line is secured by your house, so the maximum amount you can borrow depends partly on your equity in the house —i.e., its market value minus what you still owe on your mortgage. The lender will do an appraisal to determine the current value of the house.

But you must meet income and credit requirements, too. Lenders consider your income, your outstanding debts, and your credit record because they want to be certain you're able to repay the loan. Yes, it's secured by your house—but no bank *wants* to foreclose on you.

**NOTE:** Do a lot of comparison shopping.

The home equity loan market is extremely competitive—and there's a lot of variety out there, because these loans are less standardized than first mortgages. Interest rates and terms differ widely from one lender to another. "Leave no stone unturned," advises Keith Gumbinger, an analyst at HSH Associates, a mortgage research firm in Butler, New Jersey. "Sometimes the smallest lenders have the most competitive deals. The big lenders spend a lot on marketing and they make it up with somewhat higher prices. The small lenders can't afford to take full page ads, so they compete by keeping prices down."

Here's what HSH Associates says you should ask lenders to get the best deal:

◆ **What is today's interest rate?**

◆ **What index is that based on?** Typically, lenders base their home equity line rates on the prime rate as published in *The Wall Street Journal.*

◆ **What is the margin over that index?** This is what the loan will actually cost you. Today, most lenders charge 1 to 1.5 percentage points over the prime rate. "But some lenders let you to borrow at the prime rate, with no margin," says Gumbinger.

◆ **Is there an interest rate ceiling? A floor?** Unlike adjustable-rate mortgages, the vast majority of home equity lines don't have per adjustment caps or annual caps. "There has to be a ceiling, but it doesn't have to be competitive," says Gumbinger. "Most lenders let the cap float up to the state's usury ceiling, which can be as high as 25 percent. But some lenders let you buy a cap for a fee."

◆ **Is there a term on the credit line or is it open-ended?** Most home equity lines of credit have an advance term and a repayment term. During the advance term, typically five or 10 years, you can draw on the money and you're billed every month. Some lenders let you pay interest-only during the advance term. During the repayment term, which may be 10 to 15 years, you can't borrow; you repay the loan.

◆ **Is there an advance term and a repayment term, or does the loan balloon?** Some lenders offer balloon arrangements—you can borrow *and* repay during a 10-year term, for example, at the end of which time you must repay any remaining balance in a lump sum.

◆ **Are there any points charged on the line or the**

loan? Very competitive lenders offer home equity lines of credit for no fees, Gumbinger says.

◆ **What is the maximum percentage of the house value that you'll lend**? In most cases, you can borrow on your equity up to 90 or 95 percent of the market value of the house. But some lenders let you borrow 100 percent of the value of your house.

◆ **What, if any, are the closing costs or other fees I'll be required to pay?**

◆ **Is there an annual fee? If so, how much is it?**

◆ **Are there prepayment penalties?** Increasingly, the answer is yes, especially within the first two years. (*Note:* A prepayment penalty could drive up the cost of refinancing your first mortgage, because when you refinance, you must pay off all outstanding loans against the house.)

There's a respectable tradition of tapping home equity to pay for home improvements. It can also make sense to borrow against the house to help pay the cost of a college tuition. In both cases, you're borrowing specific sums of money to make specific major purchases—and in both cases, you're making a long-term investment. A new kitchen will increase the market value of your house and a college education will increase your child's lifetime earning power.

It's a lot dicier to borrow against your house to pay for short-term purchases. Home equity loans are promoted as a way to consolidate debt into a single, tax-deductible monthly payment. But if you're already carrying more debt than you can handle, almost by definition you're not someone who should borrow against his house. A home equity loan is an opportunity to dig yourself into a deeper hole with a brand-new shovel if you aren't good at managing debt, if you tend to spend more with credit than with cash, or if you have a propensity to make minimum monthly payments and nothing more, says Gumbinger.

**NOTE:** Even at a lower interest rate, you won't save money if you convert consumer debt that you would have paid off in four years into a 10- or 15-year home equity loan. "If you're consolidating credit card debt, to benefit financially you must pay the home equity loan off in the same time frame as you'd have paid the credit card debt," says Gumbinger.

Other potential dangers:

◆ Interest rates will rise, driving the variable rate on your home equity debt higher than you ever expected.

◆ Real estate values will fall, wiping out your remaining equity. Example: Your house is worth $100,000 and you have an $80,000 mortgage. You borrow $10,000 against your equity. If the value of the house falls by 10 percent, it's worth $90,000. Your total mortgage is also $90,000. Your equity is gone.

◆ Your marriage will sour and your spouse will empty your home equity line. All it takes is one signature to borrow on this credit line.

◆ You'll be unable to move because after paying off the first and the second mortgages you won't have money enough left to make a downpayment on a new house.

## Q11 Should I refinance my mortgage?

The old rule is that you should refinance only if you can lower your interest rate by two percentage points. But it may be worth doing for less, depending on how long you plan to stay in the house.

There are drawbacks to refinancing. Even if you do it with the same lender, you'll have the same expenses and hassles as when you applied for your current mortgage. Once again, you'll pay for an appraisal, credit report, title searches, etc. (*see* **Q5**).

Ask the lender if any of the existing documents—

the survey, for example—will still pass muster. Points charged on a refinance aren't fully tax-deductible in the year you pay them, but can be amortized over the life of the loan. You can probably forgo your own lawyer this time, but you still have to pay the bank's lawyer.

Comparison shop among lenders over the telephone or on your computer (*see "Appendix"*). Add up the total cost of the best deal and divide it by the amount you'll save every month with the lower interest rate. If it costs $2,000 to refinance, for example, and you reduce your monthly payment by $200, you'll make the cost back in 10 months. Even if you plan to be in the house for only another two years, that's worthwhile: You'll recover the cost of refinancing and pocket $2,800 ($200 a month for 14 months) before you move.

## Q12 Should I consider a reverse mortgage?

*See "Retirement,"* **Q15**.

## Q13 Should I consider giving my house to my children but keeping a life estate for myself?

*See "Estate Planning,"* **Q10**.

## Q14 When I sell the house, how is my profit taxed—and how can I minimize the tax?

*See* **Q8**.

## Q15 If I sell my house at a loss, will I owe taxes on the money I receive?

No, because it isn't income. That's the good news. The bad news is that your loss on the sale of a personal residence isn't tax deductible.

CHAPTER

4

# INSURANCE

NSURANCE IS A VITALLY important part of any financial plan. It's also the hardest basic financial product to understand, and probably the most frequently overpriced. The difficulty of comparison shopping for many of their products makes it easy for insurers to overcharge.

Life insurance is a prime example. It has been common industry practice to mislead customers about the true cost and nature of the life insurance policies they're buying. If you think that's an overstatement, consider this: Within the past few years, the nation's leading life insurers, including household names like Prudential, Metropolitan Life, John Hancock, Transamerica, Phoenix Home Life, and New York Life, have agreed to pay hundreds of millions of dollars to settle class action lawsuits alleging that their agents engaged in widespread deceptive sales practices.

What can you do to protect yourself?

Buy plain-vanilla products and buy them directly from the insurer whenever possible. GEICO (auto insurance) and USAA and Ameritas (life insurance) are among the very solid companies that sell via telephone. Simple, direct-marketed products typically are both cheaper and easier to understand. (There are exceptions, of course. Don't buy any direct-marketed product on the strength of a celebrity's heartfelt TV endorsement. Those policies typically are horrendously overpriced. In fact, you should avoid any policy that's advertised as coverage for which you can't be turned down. They're all priced on the assumption that they'll attract high-risk policyholders.)

Recognize that insurance agents earn their living from sales commissions, and that commissions vary enormously depending on the type of policy you buy. If you need a complex, expensive product like cash value insurance—a combination of insurance and investment account—buy a low-load policy from a company like USAA or Ameritas, and/or enlist the assistance of a fee-only insurance adviser. *(For information on finding an insurance adviser, see "Epilogue.")*

As a policyholder, you want your insurer to be financially healthy. Look for a company with a good credit rating *(see "Appendix")*. Ironically, the fact that insurance is often overpriced doesn't necessarily mean that the company selling it is financially healthy. Many insurance companies are extremely inefficient and have high expenses.

## Q1 Do I need life insurance?

Yes—if you have financial dependents and your savings aren't enough to cover their needs if you die tomorrow.

Life insurance is a terrific way to replace your income if you die prematurely. That's why you should buy it—not to fund your retirement or your child's college education. There are better and less expensive ways to meet those goals.

True, cash value life insurance—a combination of insurance and savings account—is widely marketed as a tax-deferred investment. The policy's savings account does grow on a tax-deferred basis. But this tax-deferral is offset by the high ongoing cost of the policy. In fact, the policy cost is so high that despite the tax deferral, it typically takes *15 years* to earn more in a cash value policy than you would in a comparable taxable investment, says Glenn Daily, a fee-only insurance consultant in New York City.

Don't even consider a life insurance policy as an investment unless you're already using all your other tax-deferred investments—401(k) plan, IRA, Keogh, etc.—to the absolute maximum. Those retirement accounts all cost much less than life insurance.

You don't need life insurance if you're single and have no dependents or if your only dependent is a financially self-supporting spouse. Insurance agents often argue that you should buy a policy anyway, just in case you later become so sick that you're uninsurable. That's extremely unlikely. Fewer than 2 percent of the people who apply for life insurance are turned down.

*You also don't need life insurance if you're a child* unless you're also a movie star who supports your family. In my view, there's no greater indictment of industry sales practices than the fact that one in every four cash value policies sold in the U.S. every year covers a child under 18. Those sales are great for the salespeople; cash value coverage pays the highest commissions. They're great for the insurer; there's almost no risk a death benefit will ever be paid. But they're a waste of the parents' money.

If you want to protect your child with insurance, buy bigger policies on yourself and your spouse.

If you want to invest for your child's college education, buy no-load mutual funds. That way, your money is all going to work for your investment goal. Your return isn't reduced by sales commissions and the cost of insurance on your child's life.

Here's what I mean: Let's say you can invest $500 a year for college for your one-year-old child. Assuming that both will earn 10 percent a year after expenses, which is the better investment—a taxable no-load mutual fund or a tax-deferred mutual fund wrapped in an insurance policy? The answer: the taxable mutual fund.

If you invest $500 a year in a $150,000 variable universal life insurance policy on the child's life, its cash value might grow to $13,200 by the time he's 18 years old, says Ray Martin, vice president of Ayco, an Albany, New York, financial planning firm, and author of *Your Financial Guide*. If you invest $500 a year in a taxable stock index fund earning the same 10 percent return, you'd have more than $21,000—*after* paying a 20 percent capital gains tax.

## Q2 How much life insurance do I need?

It depends on how much income you need to replace in the event of your death, and for how long.

As a very rough rule of thumb, a person with young children needs coverage equal to seven to 10 times his or her salary. A good financial planner or insurance agent can help you refine this calculation. That's important, because your real insurance needs can vary greatly depending on your specific financial situation.

The calculation must estimate both your family's future living expenses and major one-time expenditures like your funeral and your children's college education. You must supply the information that will enable your adviser to:

◆ Estimate your survivors' ongoing monthly expenses, modifying the family's current budget by any changes that would be likely after your death.

◆ Calculate what your survivors' income would be after your death. This will include your spouse's salary, any applicable Social Security survivor benefits, and any income from your investments.

◆ Multiply the monthly shortfall by 12 to get the annual shortfall.

◆ Multiply the annual shortfall by the number of years until your children are grown and/or your spouse reaches retirement age.

That's the amount of insurance you need to cover

the hole your death would leave in the family's monthly budget.

Your policy should also be big enough to cover one-time costs. These include your funeral expenses and the cost of probating your will. Your financial adviser should help you estimate these expenses. You may also want to add $10,000 of coverage for any uninsured medical bills.

Other one-time expenses include paying off your mortgage and putting your kids through college. (If you add enough coverage to pay off the mortgage, don't forget to subtract mortgage payments from the family's monthly budget.) For college, you need enough coverage to pay what it would cost today— about $7,500 a year at a public college, and $19,000 a year at a private university. (Those average annual costs include tuition, board, room, and various fees.) Your survivors can invest that amount to keep up with future cost increases—expected to average about 6 percent a year—until the kids are ready for college.

These one-time expenses will be offset by the assets you leave. They include: your savings and investment accounts, retirement plans (IRAs, Keoghs, 401(k) plans, etc.), equity in your house, lump sum pension benefit if any, plus any life insurance you already own, and any college savings plan you've already started.

Calculate the shortfall for paying these major expenses. Add it to the family budget shortfall. The total is the amount of life insurance you need.

## Q3 Should I buy term insurance or permanent insurance?

It depends on your age, on how much insurance you need, and how long you'll need it.

Life insurance comes in only two basic flavors: term

insurance and permanent insurance. Permanent insurance is also often called cash value insurance or whole life insurance.

Term insurance is protection against premature death, pure and simple. If you die while you're covered, the insurer pays your beneficiary the face amount of the policy. Term policies cover you for fixed periods of time—one, five, 10, 15, or 20 years. The policies typically are renewable until you're 80 years old. Term premiums start very low and gradually increase as you get older. But you're not locked in; you can drop the policy at any time without incurring a surrender charge (a penalty insurers levy for dropping other types of policy within a few years of purchase.) That's a big plus, because the cost of term insurance has plummeted in the past decade, enabling many people to replace their policies at lower cost every few years. Term insurance is also the only life insurance product for which you can easily comparison shop. *(For how to do this, see "Epilogue.")*

Cash value coverage combines a death benefit and a savings account whose earnings are tax-deferred. This account is called the policy's cash value. You can tap the cash value by borrowing against it at a favorable interest rate, or by surrendering the policy.

**NOTE:** At your death, your beneficiary receives only the policy's death benefit—not the death benefit and the cash value. If you die leaving outstanding policy loans and interest due, these are subtracted from the death benefit.

Cash value insurance covers you for as long as you live, which is why it's called permanent. The policy premiums start much higher than those for term insurance. A healthy 30-year-old man might pay $300 a year for a $300,000 term policy, versus $3,000 a year for the same amount of fixed-premium cash value coverage, for example. But the premiums for permanent insurance are intended to remain level for the life of the policy.

One pitch for cash value insurance is that it lets you accomplish two goals: The death benefit protects your family while your children are young; and after they're grown, you can use the policy's cash value as a source of retirement income. These policies typically are sold as investments. While the salesperson naturally talks about how the coverage will protect your loved ones in the event of your untimely death, he or she concentrates on a more upbeat scenario—i.e., the prospect that you'll live to enjoy this money yourself.

Agents also sometimes argue that because term insurance has no savings feature, if you live, you have nothing to show for all the premiums you paid. By the same reasoning, homeowners insurance is a waste of money unless your house burns down.

Your first priority with insurance is to protect your family. The reality is that very few young families can afford a cash value policy with a death benefit that's big enough to cover the cost of raising and educating the kids if one of the parents dies. Because term insurance provides maximum coverage at minimal cost, it's by far the best product for the people who need insurance the most—people who are in their twenties through their forties and have young dependents.

If your adviser recommends a cash value policy, find out how much you'd pay for a term policy that provides the same amount of coverage. Even if you're over 50, term insurance may be less expensive than a permanent policy, depending on how long you'll need the coverage.

A permanent policy may cost you less if you're over 50 and need life insurance for 15 to 20 years. You're also a candidate for permanent coverage if you'll need life insurance until you die—either because you haven't accumulated enough in other investments to provide for a nonworking spouse, for example, or because your survivors will owe big estate taxes at your death. *(For more on life insurance and estate planning, see* **Q14** *and "Estate Planning,"* **Q9***.)*

**NOTE:** Don't buy a cash value policy unless you're sure you can afford to pay the premiums for at least 15 years. Term insurance typically is so much cheaper that you would have to hold the cash value policy for 15 years before its savings account earned more than you'd make by buying a term policy and investing the premium savings in a taxable account, says Glenn Daily, a New York City insurance consultant. "That's true even for low-load [i.e., low sales commission] cash value policies," he adds.

The full sales commission on a term policy can run from 35 percent to 80 percent of the first year's premium. On a cash value policy, commissions plus other expenses often add up to 100 percent or more of a much bigger first year's premium. On a $300,000 term policy, for example, the agent could earn a $240 commission; on a $300,000 cash value policy, he might earn $1,500. You don't pay the sales commission as a separate charge; it's included in the premium cost.

Not surprisingly, agents prefer to sell permanent insurance. I still remember how my husband's former agent tried to dissuade me from buying a term policy when I was 30 years old by pointing out that its coverage would last only until I was 75. "All the statistics show you'll live much longer—and you'll be uninsured!" he cried. (When I asked why I'd need life insurance at 75, his only reply was to shake his head and say that like all New Yorkers, I was hard to argue with.)

**NOTE:** If you need term insurance now, but think you may later need permanent insurance, buy a term policy that is convertible. Most term policies let you convert to permanent coverage without further proof of good health *(see* **Q6***)*.

*(For more on buying insurance, see "Epilogue.")*

## Q4 Is this a level-term policy?

If you buy a term policy for any term longer than one year, you'll pay a level premium—i.e., a premium that stays constant for the five-, 10-, or 15- year life of the policy. If you buy annual renewable coverage, your premium will increase every year.

Level-term premiums typically start higher than annual term premiums, but are lower in the later years. If you know you'll need coverage for a specific period of time—say, only until your youngest child graduates from college in five years—it's sensible to compare the cost of five-year level-term policies with the cost of annual renewable policies over a five-year period.

In general, I prefer annual renewable policies because they offer the greatest flexibility: You're guaranteed continued coverage without another physical exam, and every year you can replace your policy with less expensive coverage if you can find it. (Obviously, if you do this, you must maintain your old policy until the replacement policy goes into effect.)

Level-term coverage is a relatively recent development. It was the insurance industry's response to the fact that the cost of term insurance has fallen steadily for the past 15 years thanks to improved mortality and better company underwriting. People in general live longer, and insurers are more skilled at identifying those likely to die sooner. As the cost of term insurance for healthy people has dropped, they have replaced their annual policies every couple of years with cheaper coverage. But if you buy a 15-year level-term policy, you have a financial incentive to keep it, since you paid a higher initial premium in order to enjoy a lower premium in later years.

## Q5 What are the terms of renewal when the original term life policy expires?

One advantage of annual renewable term is that the policy guarantees your right to annual renewal without another physical exam. Policies sold for five-, 10-, 15-, or 20-year periods typically don't let you renew coverage at the same favorable rates after the policy period ends unless you submit to another medical exam. If it turns out that your health has deteriorated—even marginally, in some cases—you'll have to pay a much higher premium to renew your coverage.

Avoid "reentry" level-term policies if there's a chance you'll still need life insurance after the policy period ends. The money you save on the initial premium isn't worth the risk that your insurance will become prohibitively expensive at the very time you need it most.

**NOTE:** If you do wind up in this bind, it may make more sense to convert your policy to permanent coverage than to renew it as expensive term coverage.

**NOTE:** Be careful not to inadvertently replace a term policy that guarantees renewability with one that doesn't.

## Q6 Is this term policy convertible to permanent coverage?

Most term policies have a conversion privilege. That means you have the option to exchange your policy for cash value coverage without another medical examination. (Naturally, you'll pay more for the cash value policy.)

In general, you should avoid term insurance that restricts your conversion option to the first few years after you buy the policy, or that permits conversion only until you reach age 60. With that kind of policy language, the insurer is only on the hook to cover you while you're still relatively young and healthy. A restricted option to switch to a cash value policy typically terminates at the very point in time when it would become most valuable to you.

## Q7 Have I been quoted 'preferred rates'?

Whether you're buying term or permanent insurance, the preferred rate is what you'll pay if your health is excellent, you're a nonsmoker, your weight is within insurance company guidelines for your height, and you don't engage in any activities the insurer considers high-risk, like sky-diving or flying an airplane.

The specific criteria for preferred rates vary from one company to another. About 90 percent of policyholders are considered average risks and pay standard premiums. If you have been quoted a preferred rate, that's nice—but it's not official until you've completed the policy application and had a medical examination. So find out what the standard premium is, too.

If you're being treated for a medical condition—

hypertension, for example, or diabetes—ask whether that will affect your premium. The answer will vary depending on the insurer.

**NOTE:** Don't lie about your medical history. In this computerized age, you can't get away with it; big pieces of your medical record, if not all of it, are easily accessible to insurers. If the insurer finds out you lied, it can substantially reduce the benefit paid to your survivors or deny coverage altogether.

Comparison shopping is just as important if you're in poor health as it is if you're in excellent health. Rate classifications aren't standardized—the assessment of medical risk varies from insurer to insurer. Some insurers quote better rates than others for people who are overweight, or are recovering alcoholics, or have histories of heart disease. A company that keeps abreast of medical advances in cardiac care, for example, will quote better rates for people with a history of heart problems because it believes it can identify those who'll live longer.

**NOTE:** If you have health problems or a family history of poor health, call your state insurance department and/or one of the insurance agencies listed in the epilogue and ask to be referred to insurers who specialize in 'impaired risk' coverage.

## Q8 What's the financial strength of this insurance company?

This matters a lot. You don't want your insurer to expire before you do.

Even if you're buying annual renewable term, the insurance company's financial health is important. If the insurer goes out of business, you'll have to look for replacement coverage unless regulators transfer your policy to another company; if your health has deteriorated, you may have to pay a substantially higher premium.

With a cash value policy, the insurer's long-term reliability is even more essential: you're trusting this company to hold and invest your savings until you die.

An insurer's ability to honor its obligations is reflected in credit ratings from A.M. Best & Co., Standard & Poor's, Moody's, and Duff & Phelps. Ask your adviser to provide ratings from all four agencies for any insurer you're considering. You can also obtain the ratings yourself in the reference section of most public libraries, or over the telephone from the agencies themselves (see "Appendix").

But be warned: Credit ratings are not a guarantee. It's worth noting that the three big life insurers that have run aground since 1991—Executive Life, Mutual Benefit Life, and Confederation Life—had excellent ratings from at least one major rating agency just months before they failed. That's why you should stick to insurers that have good ratings from at least three of the four big rating agencies.

## Q9 If I need permanent insurance, what kind should I buy?

There are three major types of permanent insurance: whole life, universal life, and variable life.

All three give you a death benefit and a tax-deferred savings account called the cash value, which you get back if you surrender the policy. (When you do this, you'll owe taxes on any amount that exceeds the premiums you paid.) You can also use the cash value as collateral for a loan at a favorable interest rate. Any loans and interest that are outstanding at your death will be deducted from the benefit paid to your survivors.

**NOTE:** If you surrender a policy within a few years of buying it, chances are you'll get very little cash back. Cash value grows very slowly in the early years. Many policies also impose surrender fees—i.e., a penalty if you drop the policy within a few years after buying it.

Ask your adviser what you'd get if you surrendered any policy you're considering after five years. This is an important question: Industry statistics show that 50 percent of the people who buy cash value coverage drop it within seven years. Don't buy any cash value policy whose surrender value at the end of one year is less than 50 percent of the premium, says James Hunt, a life insurance actuary, former state insurance commissioner, and director of the Consumer Federation of America's insurance group.

Whole life is the most basic type of cash value policy. The premium stays fixed for the life of the policy and part of it buys a fixed death benefit. The rest goes into a savings account. In some whole-life policies, your savings account earns a fixed rate that changes periodically; others pay a fluctuating rate pegged to a specific benchmark, like the return on three-month Treasury bills. Whole-life policies typically guarantee a minimum rate of 4 percent to 5 percent.

Universal life combines an adjustable death benefit with a savings account. The savings account pays an interest rate similar to what you'd earn on short- to intermediate-term Treasuries. Within set parameters, you can increase or reduce your premium payments after the policy is in effect, in order to change your death benefit, or to change the amount going into the savings account every month. (In most policies, if you want to increase the death benefit, you'll have to undergo another medical exam.)

**NOTE:** If your earnings in a universal policy savings account don't cover the cost of its death benefit, your cash value will go down. Eventually, it may disappear. If that happens, your policy will terminate unless you pay higher premiums or reduce your death benefit. Insurers don't always give you timely warning that this is happening.

Variable life insurance can be bought for fixed premiums or flexible premiums. It combines a flexible death benefit with a savings account that can be shifted at your direction among a choice of mutual fund investments. Variable policies don't guarantee a minimum return on investment; their cash value can go down as well as up. In most cases, if your investments perform very badly, your premiums will go up to maintain the guaranteed death benefit. If they perform very well, your death benefit can go up.

Variable policies typically are expensive. They carry hefty surrender charges and high administrative expenses and investment management fees *(see "Investing,"* **Q14***)*. To overcome this expense hurdle, your investment really has to be in stock funds or high-yield (i.e., junk) bonds for 15 years or more, says Glenn Daily. If you're more comfortable investing your life insurance account in a fixed-income or money market fund, you should buy a whole-life or universal policy.

If you're considering a variable policy, the available menu of investments—the number, diversity, and performance track record of the mutual funds you can select—is of the first importance. You don't want a policy that limits you to a small menu of mediocre funds.

Consider variable insurance only if all the following statements are true:

◆ You need permanent coverage.

◆ You're comfortable with the idea of taking investment risk in your life insurance policy.

◆ You have enough discretionary income to pay higher premiums to maintain your coverage if your investments underperform.

◆ You intend to hold the policy for at least 15 years.

◆ You already take full advantage of your 401(k) plan and any other tax-deferred retirement accounts available to you.

### Q10 What's the advantage of low-load life insurance?

Your cash value grows much faster in a low-load policy.

Your premium for any permanent policy must cover three basic costs: the insurer's expenses, including administrative fees and sales commission; the policy's death benefit; and your cash value investment account.

On most cash value policies, the initial expenses are so high that very little money is left to go into the investment account. On a fully loaded policy, the agent's commission and other sales costs can add up to 100 percent or more of your first year's premium. People who drop permanent coverage after only a few years are often shocked to discover that they get little or no money back from the policy's cash value account, despite the very high premiums they've paid.

By contrast, the sales expenses on a low-load policy are about 15 percent to 25 percent of the first year's premium. If you walk away from a low-load policy early on, you'll get back most of the money you put into it.

Here's an example—a comparison of two $100,000 universal life policies sold in 1986, one from Phoenix Home Life Insurance Co. and the other from USAA Life Insurance Co. On both policies, the premium was $1,500: After one year, the full-commission policy from Phoenix Home Life had zero cash value, says New York City insurance consultant Glenn Daily. The low-load USAA policy had a $1,296 cash value. *(For information on how to buy low-load life insurance, see "Epilogue.")*

## Q11 If I already own the wrong type of permanent policy, should I drop it and buy another kind?

Not unless you have reason to think the insurer is in financial trouble—and even then, only after getting advice from an adviser who has no financial interest in your decision.

You can often save money by changing *term* policies. But replacing permanent life insurance is a very expensive proposition because the policy's biggest expenses are charged in the early years. You don't get that money back when you drop the coverage—and you'll pay the same big upfront expenses all over again in a new policy. If you're older or your health has changed, you'll pay higher premiums for new policy, too.

If you've held the policy long enough to build a substantial cash value, dropping it will also trigger a tax bill. To the extent that policy earnings exceed your premiums, they're taxable when withdrawn.

The one person sure to benefit from the purchase of any new permanent policy is the agent who sells it. Policy churning—i.e., encouraging people to cash in or borrow against an old policy in order to buy a new, more expensive policy—is one of the misleading sales practices alleged in class action suits settled by the nation's largest life insurers.

A reliable and affordable source of advice on whether or not to replace a cash value policy is James Hunt, an insurance actuary at the Consumer Federation of America *(see **Q12** and "Epilogue")*.

## Q12 How can I expect this cash value policy to perform for me?

A good adviser will clearly explain to you what's guaranteed in your policy and what is not.

Every insurer provides illustrations of what a policy will be worth in future years, but these illustrations are merely a best-case scenario that isn't guaranteed.

The illustrations are a projection based on the company's assumptions about its own future expenses and investment returns, its future mortality experience (i.e., how frequently policyholders will die), and its future policy lapses (i.e., how often people will drop policies before the insurer has recouped the cost of selling them.)

Since the illustration is a sales tool, these assumptions are often grossly unrealistic. Moreover, they vary from one insurer to another. It's impossible for the average person to comparison shop for cash value coverage. The illustration for Policy A may boast much lower premiums and higher cash values down the road than the illustration for Policy B—but that may mean that Insurer A is a cockeyed optimist and/or heavily invested in high-yield, high-risk instruments, and that Insurer B is prudently conservative.

The only valid comparisons are of past performance. If the company and/or agent can't provide actual performance history on this policy for the past 10 years, look for another company and agent.

The most basic questions to ask your adviser are:

♦ What are the policy's minimum *guaranteed* cash value and death benefit?

♦ What interest rates has the insurer actually credited to the policy's cash value for each of the past 10 years? What is the future interest rate assumed in the policy illustration?

**NOTE:** Some agents use policy illustrations based on rates the insurer hasn't paid for years. In today's low interest rate environment, for example, it's unrealistic for an insurer to assume future annual returns in the double-digits.

◆ Are the policy's projected cash value and death benefit based on the insurer's *current* expenses, policy lapse experience, and dividend payments—or on future improvements in some or all of these factors?

**NOTE:** After buying a cash value policy, ask your adviser to give you an 'in-force' policy illustration every year. In-force illustrations show what your policy will be worth in the future assuming a continuation of the insurer's current expenses, mortality and policy lapse experience, and invest-ment returns.

**NOTE:** You can buy a disinterested analysis of any cash value policy from the Consumer Federation of America. The analysis is done by James Hunt, an actuary and former state insurance commissioner. He crunches the numbers for you and provides written commentary explaining what they mean; the cost is $40 for the first policy illustration and $30 for each additional illustration you submit at the same time. (For more information, write to CFA, 1424 16th Street, N.W., Suite 604, Washington, DC 20036, or call 202-387-6121.)

## Q13 Do my future premiums depend on what hap-pens to interest rates?

Policy illustrations sometimes suggest that eventually your insurance premiums will vanish. This assumption is often unwarranted.

The basic idea is that you'll no longer have to pay premiums to maintain your policy because its cash value will be so big it will generate enough investment income to cover the premiums.

Whether this will actually happen depends on whether the insurer's assumptions about future interest rates are correct. If not, you may have to pay premiums longer—perhaps indefinitely—to maintain your coverage.

Ask your adviser what happens to your premium payments under different interest rate scenarios. What will happen if interest rates drop after you've stopped paying premiums, for example? Insurers' projections during the 1980s were based on the assumption that double-digit interest rates would continue indefinitely. Instead, interest rates fell. The result: Many people have to pay premiums for a lot longer than they expected in order to maintain their policies.

### Q14 Should my spouse and I consider a second-to-die policy?

Not unless you own substantially more than $1.2 million in assets and they're in an illiquid form—such as real estate, an art collection, or a closely held business—or you're dealing with a special need, like funding a trust for a disabled child.

Ask your advisers if your estate is likely to owe estate taxes when you die. If so, will your liquid assets will be enough to pay those taxes? If the answer is no, a second-to-die policy is one potential solution. Another would be to take steps to reduce your estate taxes *(see "Estate Planning," Q7)*.

A second-to-die policy is designed for married couples and is primarily used to pay estate taxes. The policy covers two people, but the death benefit is paid only at the second death. Estate taxes typically aren't due until then, because there's an unlimited tax exemption on assets that one spouse leaves to the other.

Let's say a couple has $4 million in assets, of which their family business represents more than $2 million. By taking full advantage of the $600,000 estate tax exemption available to every taxpayer, together they can shelter up to $1.2 million from estate taxes. *(For an explanation of how to do this, see "Estate Planning.")* Starting in 1998, small business owners and farm owners will be able to choose between this $600,000 personal estate tax exemption—which will rise gradually over the next 10 years to $1 million—and a new $1.3 million small business estate tax exemption. But that still leaves a taxable estate.

When a closely held business represents more than 35 percent of your adjusted gross estate, your heirs have the option to pay the taxes that are attributable to the business in installments over a 14-year period, says Jeff Saccacio, West Coast partner in charge of personal financial services at Coopers & Lybrand. "Paying taxes on installment is preferable to liquidating the business, but it's very expensive because interest is due on the tax payments, too," says Saccacio.

A better option would be for you and your spouse to set up an irrevocable life insurance trust as the owner of your second-to-die policy. When the surviving spouse dies, the policy proceeds are paid to the trust, which can then lend his or her estate the money to pay the taxes. The estate pays interest on the loan to the trust, whose beneficiaries are your heirs.

But remember, life insurance doesn't reduce your estate taxes—it merely provides money to pay them. The policy isn't inexpensive, especially if you're over 50 and in less than perfect health. You don't need this coverage if you'll leave enough liquid assets to pay the taxes due on your estate. If not, you should consider ways to reduce your estate tax, like making gifts during your lifetime. You'll get more pleasure from giving money to your children, grandchildren, and favorite charities than you'd ever get from enriching an insurance company.

Finally, if you decide to buy a second-to-die policy, neither of you should own it. It should be owned by an irrevocable life insurance trust or by your children *(see "Estate Planning")*.

## Q15 Do I need disability insurance?

Yes, if your paycheck is your main source of income and you don't have adequate group disability coverage at work.

Disability insurance pays you a monthly benefit if you can't work. It's protection against the risk that you'll be unable to earn a living because of a serious injury. This protection is particularly important if your salary is the main source of income in your household. A good policy will replace up to 60 percent of your earnings. The cost depends on your age, health, occupation, and on the policy's terms and conditions.

Statistically, your risk of a disabling injury is greater than your risk of premature death. But many more people own life insurance than disability insurance. One reason is that disability policies are expensive; you can easily pay $2,000 a year or more for a policy that replaces $50,000 of annual income. Another reason is that it's easier to envision being killed instantly in a car crash than surviving 30 years in a wheelchair.

You may already have some disability coverage through your job. Big employers typically provide two kinds: Short-term group disability usually covers you for 30 days to six months. Long-term group disability coverage kicks in after 180 days. Typically, it pays you for two years if you can't work in your own occupation, and thereafter only if you can't work at all. Sometimes the employer pays for group disability coverage;

sometimes the cost is split between the employer and the employees; sometimes, it's available only if you pick up the tab yourself.

**NOTE:** Find out what your employer provides and ask to pay the premiums yourself through payroll deduction. The reason: if you pay the premiums, any benefits you collect under the policy will be tax exempt. If your employer pays the premiums, the benefits are taxable income.

The cost you pay for group coverage depends on your age and occupation as well as the policy's covered compensation limit, says Barry Barnett, a principal at Kwasha Lipton Group of Coopers & Lybrand, LLP, a Fort Lee, New Jersey, employee benefits consultant. Let's say the group plan pays 50 percent of salary up to $5,000 a month. In other words, to collect the full $5,000 a month, you must earn $10,000 a month, or $120,000 a year. The covered compensation limit is therefore $120,000. For a white collar worker in his or her mid-thirties, the insurance in this example would cost 0.25 percent to 0.35 percent of the covered compensation limit—or about $300 to $420 a year.

Workers compensation pays disability benefits for injuries sustained on the job; the amount paid depends on state law and on your earnings. The average weekly maximum payment under workers comp is now about $450. Most states require lifetime payments in cases of permanent total disability.

Social Security also pays long-term disability benefits to eligible workers with disabilities that are expected to last at least one year and prevent them from doing any substantial gainful work—but it's extremely tough to qualify for these benefits. In 1995, 61 percent of the people who applied for them were turned down.

Be prepared to tell your adviser the amount and terms of any coverage you already have at work, as well as your household expenses and current income, including your spouse's earnings and any investment income you have. The shortfall is the amount of individual disability insurance you need to buy.

**NOTE:** Some group disability policies reduce the benefit they pay by any benefit that you receive from an individual policy you purchased later, says Barnett. If you're already covered by this kind of group policy, buying additional coverage in an individual policy is a waste of money. But if you can buy the individual policy before joining the group policy, Barnett says, you can get full benefits from both.

## Q16 How long has the insurer been selling disability coverage?

Buy your policy from an established disability insurer like Northwestern Mutual, Paul Revere, Unum, or Provident Life & Accident.

These four companies account for more than 50 percent of the market in disability insurance. They're likelier to keep upgrading policies and to pay promptly than an insurer for whom disability insurance is a sideline or a new venture. If you have to file a claim, you might have a 40-year relationship with your disability insurer—you want one that's committed to staying in the market.

## Q17 How much protection does the policy provide?

Understanding the policy's language is crucial.

Ask your adviser how the policy defines disability—i.e., when do you qualify to receive benefits? How long do you have to wait after becoming disabled to start receiving payments? How long will benefits continue?

Some policies consider you disabled if you're unable to work in your own occupation. Other, much less expensive policies, pay a benefit only if you can't work at *any* job. The best compromise is an income-replacement policy: If you're disabled and can't earn your old salary, this policy brings your income up to your former compensation level regardless of your job.

In any policy, there's a waiting period between the onset of disability and the start of benefits. It's like a deductible. The longer the waiting period, the lower your premium. Pick the longest waiting period you can afford, based on sources of income other than your wages. Would your savings be enough to replace your salary for six months? Then take a six-month waiting period.

Look for coverage that will continue at least until you turn 59 and a half, when you'll be able to start tapping your retirement plans without incurring an early withdrawal penalty—or until age 65, at which point you'll be eligible for Medicare and Social Security.

**NOTE:** The cost of your policy will depend in part on whether it is 'noncancelable' or 'guaranteed renewable'. This sounds like the same thing, but it isn't. With a guaranteed renewable policy, the insurer can increase your premiums along with those of all its other policyholders, if state regulators agree. A noncancelable policy guarantees that your premiums will never rise. You pay about 20 percent more for that assurance. Don't even consider a noncancelable policy unless you're sure you can comfortably afford the premiums.

Because disability insurance is expensive, you should go for the most basic, no-frills coverage you can get. Forget the extras that substantially increase the premium, like special provisions that agree to return part of your premium if you don't become disabled. And shop for a low-load policy. *(For how to do that, see "Epilogue.")*

## Q18 Should I buy long-term care insurance?

For most people, I think the answer is no.

You shouldn't even consider this coverage unless you can afford to spend about 5 percent of your income on the premiums for many years to come and have at least $300,000 of assets you want to preserve for your heirs—and even then, I'd hesitate to buy a policy I didn't expect to need for more than a decade.

Long-term care insurance is relatively new. It pays a fixed, daily dollar benefit—typically from $50 to $150 a day—for long-term care in a nursing home or in your own home. There's a waiting period before coverage begins—a delay during which you'll have to pay for this care yourself. The longer the waiting period, the lower the premium. The best policies cover both custodial care (assistance with daily activities such as dressing and eating, for example) and skilled nursing care. Some policies also cover extra services like adult day-care centers and speech therapy.

Premiums are based on your age when you buy the insurance, and are intended to stay level as long as you own it. (Although the insurer can't single one policyholder out for premium increases, with a green light from regulators it can raise premiums for all policyholders.) A 50-year-old might pay only $400 a year for a basic policy that pays a $100-a-day benefit. A 75-year-old might pay $2,500 to $3,000 a year for the same policy. If you buy a policy that meets a federal standard, the premiums are tax-deductible to the extent that their cost exceeds 7.5 percent of your adjusted gross income, and benefits you receive are tax-free up to $175 per day ($63,875 per year) or the actual annual cost of services minus the reimbursement, whichever is greater.

There is a very clear need for this kind of insurance: Most Americans now can expect to live long enough to need ongoing assistance with bathing and dressing—not to mention grocery-shopping, cooking, and doing the laundry (services not covered by long-term care policies). And unlike previous generations, most of us can't expect that kind of daily care to be provided by family members. Most families are scattered across the United States and women who were the traditional care givers are now in the workforce.

A year in a nursing home costs about $40,000 on average, and more than $80,000 in some parts of the country—and this cost is not covered by Medicare or by private health insurance. Nursing home care *is* covered by Medicaid—but you aren't eligible for Medicaid until you've exhausted your own assets *(see "Estate Planning,"* **Q10***)*.

Nevertheless, long-term care insurance has big potential problems:

◆ The fixed premiums now being charged are based on insurers' estimates of future claims—but these estimates are unsupported by past experience or actuarial data. The coverage is so new that insurers haven't yet had any statistically meaningful claims experience. Moreover, past incidence of nursing home use is a very poor guide to future use. All the changes that created a need for long-term care insurance—the aging of the U.S. population, longer life expectancies, the shortage of family caregivers, and indeed the policy's very existence—make it a certainty that people will use nursing homes a great deal more in the future than they did in the past.

It's quite likely that today's cost estimates are too

low. If so, future long-term care insurance premiums will soar or insurers will go bankrupt—either way, a grim prospect for the policyholders.

◆ **Coverage is affordable only if you buy it many years before you actually use it.** The policy pays a fixed benefit whose value will shrink with inflation. At age 50, you buy a policy that pays a $100 daily benefit. But you probably won't use the policy until you're 80 or older. What will $100 be worth then? And will the insurer be as reliable in 30 years as it is today? Will it still be be backing the policy—or will it have sold its long-term care business to another insurer?

◆ **Future government programs may make your policy obsolete long before you need it.** Admittedly, this doesn't seem likely at the moment. The federal government has recently indicated that it doesn't intend to foot the bill for long-term care for anyone who can afford to pay for it *(see "Estate Planning," **Q10**)*. But a lot can change in a couple of decades.

## Q19 If I decide to buy long-term care insurance, does it make sense to buy the coverage through my job?

Not necessarily. Don't buy group coverage without comparison shopping to make sure it's really a good deal.

An increasing number of big companies now make it possible for their employees to buy long-term care coverage on a group basis. But your employer won't necessarily have scrutinized the policy's fine print, since he's not paying for it. And group coverage is priced to include older and sicker people as well as the young and healthy.

Compare its cost and terms with what's available in individual coverage.

**NOTE:** Long-term care policy language can vary considerably from one company to another. State laws affecting the coverage vary, too. To comparison shop, you need an agent or a financial planner who specializes in this product and is familiar with Medicare, Medicaid, geriatric-care managers, and your state's laws on issues relating to the elderly. To find one, call your local agency on aging. Most states also run free health-insurance counseling programs that provide information on long-term care insurance.

**NOTE:** If you decide to buy group coverage, make sure you could keep the policy if you left the job—and find out whether your premium would change under those circumstances.

### Q20 If I decide to shop for long-term care coverage, what should I look for?

An insurer with a good credit rating from at least three of the four big rating agencies—A.M. Best, Standard & Poor's, Moody's, and Duff & Phelps (*see "Appendix"*). The best policy in the world won't be worth anything if the insurer is out of business when you file your first claim.

You should also look for an insurer with long-term care expertise. If the company has a staff of geriatric-care managers, for example, it's a good sign that it's committed to this market. Leading long-term care insurers currently include CNA, John Hancock, and Travelers.

Avoid companies that don't require a physical examination and a physician's statement along with your application, says Deena Katz, a Coral Gables, Florida, financial planner who's an expert in this coverage. A company with tough underwriting standards will have healthier policyholders and lower premiums.

But you should also be wary of an insurer with premiums that are substantially lower than those of its competitors: when long-term care policies are underpriced, future premium increases are a certainty. The policy may become unaffordable just as you reach the age when you actually need to use it.

A good basic policy provides at least $100 a day after a 100-day waiting period, says Katz, and covers care at many types of facilities—nursing homes, custodial care residences, and adult day-care centers, as well as home health care. The waiting period is like a deductible; the longer it is, the lower your premium. The waiting period should be as long as you could afford to pay for long-term care yourself out of your own savings.

Policies are available for periods lasting from two years to your lifetime. The average stay in a nursing home is 90 days; people who stay longer, on average stay another two and a half years. Katz advises clients to look for at least three years of total coverage, half of it available for home health care.

The policy limit—the maximum you'll be paid during the life of the policy—should be expressed in dollars, not in days of care. If the policy pays up to $100 a day, for example, and you spend only $50 a day, the unused $50 should extend your available coverage.

**NOTE:** Many policies pay only half as much for home care as for institutional care. Look for coverage that pays the same daily benefit for both, says Katz. "But look for something that will fit your economic and personal circumstances," she adds. "If you're an elderly man who knows he won't be able to stay at home, you don't need a big home health care provision. If you're a woman looking for coverage for her mother, the home health care provision is important to you."

**NOTE:** Make sure the policy covers *all types* of care at all facilities. You don't want one that covers custodial care (like assistance with eating or dressing) at custodial care facilities but not at skilled nursing homes, for example.

Ask what triggers the coverage. Most policies start paying benefits (after the waiting period) if you need help with two of five activities of daily living, such as eating and dressing.

**NOTE:** Policy language should make it clear that benefits will be paid even if you're physically able to perform these daily activities, but need supervision or assistance because of cognitive impairment.

You can buy inflation protection. Some policies let you increase your benefit every three years to keep pace with the Consumer Price Index. Your premium goes up, too, of course. The alternative is a policy in which your benefit is automatically increased by a 5 percent compounded annual rate; your initial premium is much higher, but remains level.

Which is better? "It depends on whether you want to pay for inflation upfront or as you go," says Katz. "The index option policy is much cheaper to start with, but you'll have a surprise every three years when it goes up." Of course, you don't have to exercise the option to increase coverage, but if you don't, you won't keep up with inflation.

## Q21 Does the policy have a nonforfeiture clause?

If it doesn't, the premiums won't be tax-deductible.

Nonforfeiture guarantees that even if you stop paying premiums, you'll receive a reduced daily benefit after you've held the policy for a specified time period. The nonforfeiture clause also guarantees that your heirs will get back part of your premiums if you haven't used the policy. In some states, you can't buy a policy that doesn't contain a nonforfeiture clause.

Katz isn't crazy about exercising the nonforfeiture option because it makes these already pricey policies more expensive. "To me, long-term care is like fire insurance," she says. "You buy every year, and if don't have a fire, you don't need it."

CHAPTER

5

# Estate
## PLANNING

ESTATE PLANNING has two basic goals: **1)** to make sure that when you die, your assets will go to your family and friends rather than to federal and state tax collectors; and **2)** to make sure that what you own is distributed as you wish.

People who are obsessed with avoiding taxes—and that's a lot of people—tend also to be fascinated by estate planning. A large part of my mail from readers asks questions about various types of trusts that are promoted as a way to reduce estate taxes. But most trusts are designed to solve the problems of the very wealthy. They're of little or no use to most people. The only estate plan *everybody* really needs is a will—and unfortunately, three out of four Americans don't have one.

A will is a vital part of any personal financial plan—and not just because it can reduce taxes.

Its primary function is even more important: A will is the only way you can safeguard the security of the people you love.

The conventional wisdom is that most people don't draw up wills because they're afraid to face their own mortality. Larry Elkin, a financial planner in Hastings-on-Hudson, New York, disagrees: "People are reluctant, sometimes terrified, to contemplate a loved one's death—but not their own," he says. "I think people don't have wills because they're afraid of making difficult choices."

Making a will typically involves hard decisions, like picking a guardian for your children or choosing between the potentially competing financial claims of people you love. But the people you care about are much better served if you make those decisions. If you don't, your survivors are likely to waste a lot of emotional energy, time, and money fighting about what you would have wanted.

## Q1 Do I need a will?

Yes. It's the only way you get to decide what happens to everything you own when you die.

Whether you're married or single, wealthy or poor, you can't assume that your nearest and dearest will automatically inherit what you leave. If you die without a will, your state's intestacy law determines what happens to your belongings. Very often, the law's provisions are not what you would have wanted—and sometimes, they can saddle your survivors with major problems that could easily have been avoided.

Under most state intestacy laws, for example, assets that were held solely in your name are divided between your surviving spouse and children—including your children by previous marriages. This often means your surviving spouse winds up with only half of the assets you owned. The kids inherit the rest— and this isn't just a technicality. Until they attain legal majority (age 18 in most states), the children's inheritance will be administered by a court-appointed trustee. There will, of course, be a fee for this service, set by the court and based on the size of the inheritance. And that's not all: Your surviving spouse will need the court-appointed trustee's okay to tap the children's money for their needs—dental bills, summer camp, school tuition, etc.

In some states, if you die childless and without a will, your surviving spouse shares your estate with your parents. Even a childless couple who own everything jointly need wills. "I remember a childless couple who jointly owned a substantial business and had no wills," says Ed Slott, a Rockville Centre, New York tax accountant. "They died in a car crash. She was killed instantly. He survived her by two hours, inheriting the jointly held assets. When he died, under the intestacy law his parents got everything. Her whole family was disinherited."

Unmarried couples need wills even more than married couples, because they have no legal right to inherit from each other. Intestacy laws guarantee that your spouse and/or children will get at least part of your estate if you die without a will. But lovers, friends, and companions have no intestacy rights.

Finally, anyone with children needs a will. A will is the document in which you name a guardian who'll be responsible for raising your children, create a trust to hold their inheritance (minor children can't own assets), and name a trustee to manage the money. A trust is a legal entity that can own assets to be used only as designated by the creator of the trust. Money you leave in trust for your children will be used to bring them up; as the trust beneficiaries, they'll inherit any remaining balance at the age you specify.

**NOTE:** You don't have to hire a lawyer to draw up a will, but don't be seduced by the idea that you can save time and trouble by writing your will in your own simple words. If you forgo a lawyer, be sure to use legal forms (available at any legal stationer's) and a good self-help book or software. (Nolo Press sells excellent books and software on will making (see "Appendix"). To order from Nolo Press, call 800-992-6656 or visit their Web site at www.nolo.com.)

The technical jargon used in wills has very precise legal meaning; a will in ordinary English is much likelier to be open to several interpretations. Expert help also ensures that you'll cover all contingencies. On your own, for example, would you realize it's important to name a backup guardian for your kids in case your first choice dies a couple of weeks after you do?

**NOTE:** When you prepare your will, you should also review your named beneficiaries on all your financial accounts. No matter what your will says, your life insurance, retirement accounts, and bank accounts that are in trust for someone else all pass directly to the named beneficiary. If you've forgotten whom you named, call the institution holding the account and ask. You can change your named beneficiaries whenever you wish.

## Q2 Who should act as the executor?

Choose an executor the way you'd choose a business partner.

The executor is the person legally responsible for carrying out the instructions in your will. He or she is also legally responsible for overseeing everything that must be done as a result of your death—from discontinuing your telephone service and collecting your mail if you lived alone to paying your debts and taxes and locating all your assets and distributing them to your heirs. This is a demanding job and state law provides for executors to be paid *(see* **Q5***)*.

Your executor files your estate's income tax return; the estate is a separate taxpayer from the date of your death until final distribution of your assets. Whether or not estate taxes are due as well as income taxes depends on the total value of the estate. Your executor may have to have assets appraised to determine that value. If extra cash is needed to pay taxes, bequests, and debts, it's the executor who decides what assets should be sold.

Ask your lawyer if the state you live in restricts your choice of executor. In some states you can't name an out-of-state executor who is not a family member or a primary beneficiary under your will, for example.

The ideal executor is eminently trustworthy, already

familiar with your personal and financial affairs, lives nearby, has first-rate organizational abilities and plenty of common sense, and is sensitive enough to respond sympathetically to your bereaved family.

Anyone that fits this description is probably also a primary beneficiary in your will. Most people designate their spouse as executor or coexecutor. Executors who are family members often hire legal help, but the executor is legally responsible for any work he or she delegates.

You can make this person's job much easier by leaving a letter of instructions that says where you keep your important papers and provides a detailed list of all your assets, including your bank and securities accounts, retirement plans, and insurance policies. The letter should also include the names, addresses, and telephone numbers of your financial advisers. Make three extra copies: one for your attorney, one for your safe deposit box, and one for yourself.

**NOTE:** The executor named in your will isn't legally bound to accept the job, so it's a good idea to name one or two alternates.

## Q3 What should I consider in naming a guardian for my kids?

His or her ability to raise your children as you would want.

You're under no obligation to pick a blood relative as your child's guardian if you think a friend's views about raising children are closer to your own. But you must make sure whomever you choose is willing to accept the responsibility.

Don't leave money intended for the child to the guardian. Leave it in a trust for the child. You'll also have to name a trustee—not necessarily the same person as the guardian. The trustee doesn't have to be an investment professional, but should be astute enough to choose and monitor good financial advisers.

If you're extremely wealthy, you can create a trust for each of your children. If your estate is more modest, create a single "pot" trust to be maintained until all your children reach age 21. "That way, you make sure all the children are provided for until they reach adulthood," says Benjamin T. White, a partner at Alston & Bird, an Atlanta law firm.

Depending on the duration of the trust, White suggests giving each child the right to serve as co-trustee for his or her share after turning 21. "That gives the child the opportunity to gain some experience and responsibility," he says. It's prudent to specify that the senior co-trustee must sign off on all major decisions, however—just to ensure that your 21-year-old doesn't blow a small fortune in ill-advised investments.

The guardian and the trustee typically aren't the same person, says White, because the jobs require very different skills. If your best friend is great with kids but not with money, or if you want your sister to be your children's guardian, but don't think her husband is a good money manager, you can name a second person as the trustee. Alternatively, you could name an institutional trustee like a bank. But if you do that, White suggests you also name an individual as a co-trustee—and give him or her the power to fire and replace the institution if it's not doing a good job.

**NOTE:** The trustee will have to respond to economic conditions you can't foresee, so don't put investment restrictions in the trust document. State laws used to emphasize that a trustee's first priority should be preservation of capital, for example. The unfortunate result was that trustees often invested far too conservatively to keep up with inflation. In the past few years, many of these laws have been rewritten to give trustees more leeway in choosing investments and to encourage them to seek professional investment help.

### Q4 How often do I need to update my will? And where should I keep it?

It's a good idea to review your will periodically. Even if your life hasn't changed that much, there's a good chance that the tax laws have. (In fact, the most recent tax act was signed into law on August 5, 1997. If your assets are worth more than $600,000, ask your tax and legal advisers if you need to revise your will. *See* **Q7**.)

A will that's crafted to take advantage of an old law may lose the advantages of a new one. A classic example is the law that lets you leave unlimited assets tax-free to your spouse, passed in September 1981. A will dated earlier, depending on how it's worded, might not qualify for the unlimited marital deduction, says John Dadakis, a partner at Rogers & Wells in New York City.

You can keep your will in a fireproof box at home, at your lawyer's office, or in a bank safe deposit box. (But check the bank's rules first to make sure your executor would have no problem opening the box after your death. In most cases, a safe deposit box is sealed automatically at your death, but your survivors can easily obtain an order to open it.)

**NOTE:** Only the original will is considered valid. If your survivors have only a copy, they'll have to convince the court that the original was never in your possession, says Dadakis, because the law presumes that if you did have the original in your possession, it's missing because you changed your mind about its contents and destroyed it.

If you've got only a photostat of your original will, you'll save your heirs a major hassle by having a new one drawn up. It can be as simple as having your copy retyped and signed in front of new witnesses.

## Q5 How much time and money will it cost my family to settle my estate?

In television dramas, the will is read to the survivors on the afternoon of the funeral and they collect their inheritance a few days later. In real life, it may be a year until your assets are distributed to your heirs.

In fact, chances are your will won't even be located and read until several weeks after you die. You should leave instructions for your funeral arrangements in a letter to your survivors, not in your will.

Your executor generally presents your will in surrogate's court for probate within 30 days of your death. Probate is the legal validation of your will. The court officially authorizes the executor to act on behalf of your estate, and it supervises the collection and distribution of your assets. The executor takes all steps necessary to settle your estate *(see **Q2**)*. Your heirs don't receive any assets distributed under the will until this entire process is completed.

**NOTE:** Ask your lawyer if your state permits a certain amount of property to pass to your heirs free of probate. Most states do, says Jeff Saccacio, the West Coast partner in charge of Personal Financial Services for Coopers & Lybrand in Los Angeles. California, for example, provides for "a reasonable family allowance" while your assets are in probate.

Your heirs will also have immediate access to assets that never go through probate, including all your accounts with named beneficiaries (life insurance policies, retirement accounts, and bank accounts that are in trust for someone else) and accounts that you own jointly with right of survivorship. These automatically pass to the named beneficiary or surviving co-owner at your death.

The cost of probate varies from state to state. It includes court filing fees, which typically are modest, and fees to your executor and any professional advisers he or she hires—which can be steep. In California, for example, your personal representative—i.e., your executor — is allowed by law to charge 4 percent of the first $15,000 of your estate; 3 percent on the next $85,000; 2 percent of the next $900,000; 1 percent of the next $9 million; 0.5 percent on the next $15 million; and "a reasonable amount to be determined by the court" on all assets above $25 million.

But you're not bound by the fees permitted under state law. Your will can limit the executor's fee to less than the law allows, or to nothing. An executor typically waives fees in any case if he's a family member and a beneficiary under your will. But lawyers typically charge fees equal to what state law allows for the executor; and of course, they don't waive their fees.

**NOTE:** Instruct your heirs to look for an attorney who charges on an hourly basis for this job. The difficulty of settling an estate is rarely related to its size, says Scott McBride, a St. James, New York, attorney who specializes in estate planning and administration—and a fee based on the size of the estate often adds up to several times as much as the attorney's usual hourly rate. Besides, adds McBride, a percentage fee schedule may encourage the lawyer to overvalue the estate, which is the last thing you want.

## Q6 Do I need a living trust?

It depends on your age, health, and what you own.

In many states, living trusts are marketed as if no estate plan is complete without one—indeed, some hard-sell marketers imply that a living trust provides tax benefits you can't get without one. This simply isn't true. "Everything you can do with a living trust from a tax standpoint, you can also do with a well-crafted will and a power of attorney," says Jeff Saccacio.

A trust can own, buy, and sell assets just like a person. You can transfer all your assets to a living trust and still control them by making yourself a trustee; you can name trust beneficiaries who'll inherit the assets if you die. And a living trust, like a will, is revocable; you can change it as often as you wish.

There are three basic advantages to a living trust:

**1 A co-trustee can run your business and handle your personal finances if you're incapacitated**. By naming one of your children—or your bank or lawyer—a co-trustee, you make it easy for someone to take over your affairs if you become disabled or senile. You can accomplish the same thing with a durable power of attorney *(see "Marriage and Divorce,"* **Q7**).

**2 Assets in the trust avoid probate**. This can save your heirs a lot of time and red tape if your main asset is a family business, or if you own property in more than one state, says Saccacio. Otherwise, they'd have to go through the probate process in each state where you owned property.

Whether or not a living trust will also save money is much less certain. Your heirs will avoid court fees for probate, but not the legal and accounting fees which are the most significant cost of settling an estate, Saccacio points out: "They'll still need legal and accounting services, and fees for those services aren't lower if you have a living trust."

It's true that a living trust gives your heirs immediate access to your assets. But most state laws allow families immediate access to some probate assets, too, notes Saccacio *(see* **Q5***)*.

**3 Your affairs remain private after your death.** Unlike a will, a living trust isn't a public document. Your family won't be hounded by unscrupulous salespeople who know they've inherited a substantial fortune. And the general public won't be any the wiser if you leave more money to a secret lover than to your spouse. (But all your relatives will know, because potential beneficiaries are entitled to find out the provisions of the trust, says John Dadakis.)

A few caveats:

◆ **A living trust is a supplement to a will—***not a substitute*. You can't use it to name a guardian for your children, for example, and it simply isn't practical to transfer literally all your possessions into a trust. If you have no will, any property that you haven't transferred into the trust will be distributed according to your state's intestacy law *(see* **Q1***)*.

◆ **A living trust will not reduce your estate taxes or income taxes**, despite widespread belief to the contrary. You still control the assets held in the trust, so you still owe taxes on them.

◆ **Although avoiding probate saves time, it may not save money.** Lawyers typically charge more to create a living trust than a will—often upwards of $2,000.

You don't need a living trust if you own most of your assets jointly with right of survivorship, since they avoid probate anyway. You don't need a living trust if your total assets are under your state's threshold for probate; in California, for example, it's $100,000. And you probably don't need one if you're under 55 and healthy. You haven't yet acquired most of your assets; why go through the paperwork of transferring title to everything you buy every year?

If you decide you need a living trust, don't rely on a do-it-yourself kit. Have it drawn up by a lawyer familiar with your state's trust laws. The trickiest part of creating a living trust isn't writing the trust document. It's making sure that title to everything you own is properly transferred into the trust. If you do it yourself and goof, your heirs may inherit expensive problems.

**NOTE:** If you set up a perfect trust and don't complete the transfers of assets, you've wasted your time and money. "A lot of people pay $2,000 or $3,000 to set up a living trust after attending a lawyer's seminar, and then never transfer any assets into it," says Scott McBride.

## Q7 Will my estate be taxable?

It depends on what it's worth, on who will inherit it, and on the state you live in.

An estate tax is a government levy on the value of everything you own when you die—but there are important exceptions. There is no federal tax on any assets you leave to a surviving spouse who is also a U.S. citizen; to all others, you can leave up to $600,000 tax-free.

Under the 1997 tax law, this $600,000 exemption will gradually increase to $1 million over the next 10 years. The new law also gives special treatment to owners of small businesses and family farms. Starting in 1998, they're eligible for a $1.3 million federal estate tax exemption. (Qualifying business owners and farm owners will have to choose between this exemption and the personal estate tax exemption, however; they don't get both.)

**NOTE:** Even if your estate is worth less than $600,000, ask your adviser if it's subject to your state's estate taxes. State taxes kick in at much lower levels than the federal tax.

The bad news for couples who are worth more than $600,000 is that the unlimited marital estate tax exemption is really only a tax-deferral. Sure, you and your spouse can inherit everything from each other tax free—but whichever of you survives will ultimately have an estate that's federally taxable if it exceeds the nonspousal exemption.

Estate taxes are much steeper than income taxes. In 1997, they start at 37 percent on amounts over $600,000 and climb to 55 percent on amounts over $3 million. It's not as hard as you might think to exceed the $600,000 exemption. Your estate includes literally everything you own at death: the value of your house, bank, brokerage and retirement accounts, and your life insurance policies, too. If you own a $300,000 life insurance policy, for example, the beneficiaries won't owe income taxes on the proceeds—but the value of the policy will be included in your taxable estate.

**NOTE:** Ask your adviser how your retirement accounts— IRAs, 401(k)s, and Keoghs—will be taxed when you die. These accounts are subject to income taxes when the money is withdrawn by your heirs; and depending on their value, they may be subject to estate taxes as well.

One consolation: Your IRA beneficiaries are entitled to a personal income tax deduction for the portion of your estate tax that's attributable to the IRA they inherit.

## Q8 How can I reduce my estate taxes?

There are a variety of options you should discuss with your advisers. Among them:

◆ **Making gifts to your children, grandchildren, and favorite charities**. You can give up to $10,000 a year per recipient without incurring a gift tax. If you have three children and four grandchildren and give them each $10,000, for example, you've reduced your estate by $70,000. You and your spouse together could give each recipient $20,000, reducing your estate by $140,000.

**NOTE:** Over time, you can use this $10,000 annual gift tax exclusion to give away property that's worth a great deal more. Let's say you want to give your daughter and son-in-law a house worth $200,000. They give you 20 signed IOUs for $10,000, on which they pay you annual interest. Every year, you and your spouse forgive four IOUs, effectively making them a $40,000 gift. In five years, they own the house, its value is out of your estate, and you've avoided taxes on the gift.

**NOTE:** You can give to charity and keep an interest in the gift at the same time. Let's say you own highly appreciated stock; now that you're retired, you'd like to reinvest it in an asset that produces income, but you can't sell it without incurring a big capital gains tax. So instead, you give it to a charitable remainder trust—a trust with a charity as its beneficiary. The trust can sell the stock and reinvest it without being taxed, and then pay you income for life. You get a tax deduction for the value of the 'remainder interest' that will go to the charity after your death.

◆ **Creating a bypass trust in your wills**. Most married couples have wills leaving everything to each other.

This can lead to problems if you have substantial assets, because while there's an unlimited federal estate exemption on assets left to a spouse, there's only a $600,000 exemption on assets left to anyone else. (This exemption will gradually increase to $1 million over the next 10 years.) Let's say you and your spouse have a $1.2 million estate. If you both die in a common disaster, one of you will be presumed to have lived longer, if only by a few seconds, says Scott McBride. If you've left everything to each other, the person who died second is deemed to have died with a $1.2 million estate—of which $600,000 is taxable.

Instead, your wills can leave $600,000 to each other and $600,000 to a bypass trust. It pays the survivor income for life. When he or she dies, the principal goes to your children. There's no federal estate tax on their inheritance from the surviving parent or the trust, because each is less than $600,000.

**NOTE:** What if you're afraid that earmarking $600,000 for a trust might leave your surviving spouse too little to live on? Then consider a disclaimer trust instead, says McBride. It works just like a bypass trust, but it's funded only with assets that your surviving spouse chooses not to inherit after you die. As the lawyers put it, he or she "disclaims" this money. If your widow is 80 years old, for example, she might opt to disclaim $600,000, which would go into the trust. But if she's 35, she might choose not to fund the trust at all. She could opt to inherit the entire $1.2 million, figuring she'll spend most of it before she dies.

**NOTE:** If you already have a bypass trust in your will, ask your adviser if it should be rewritten to take advantage of the 1997 tax law.

◆ **Making sure someone else owns your life insurance policy, so its value isn't included in your estate.** You can transfer the policy to an irrevocable insurance trust. Since you no longer own it, its proceeds aren't included in your estate when you die. Or you can make a gift of the policy to your children.

**NOTE:** Don't wait until you're on your deathbed to give away or transfer your life insurance policy. The IRS takes a dim view of last-minute transfers: You must survive at least three years afterward, or the policy's value reverts back to your estate.

And what if you die without getting around to doing any of this? All is not lost: Your surviving spouse has up to nine months from your date of death to disclaim part of the estate he or she inherited from you. The disclaimed assets are then distributed exactly as they would have been under your will if your spouse had died first—presumably to your children. The kids thus inherit from your estate and later from your surviving spouse's estate. If both inheritances are under the exempt amount, there's no estate tax on either one.

## Q9 Does it make sense to buy life insurance to pay my estate taxes?

Probably not, unless your heirs would otherwise have to sell your house or other illiquid assets to pay the taxes *(see "Insurance,"* **Q14***)*.

If you decide you need life insurance to cover estate taxes, make sure you don't own the policy yourself. If you do, its value is included in your estate—increasing the taxes and thus aggravating the very problem you're trying to solve *(see* **Q7***)*.

## Q10 Should I consider giving my house to my kids, but keeping a life estate?

This has become a tough question to answer. Until recently, the reason people did this was to speed up their eligibility for Medicaid coverage in a nursing home. Whether or not this still makes sense hinges in part on interpretation of a clause in a 1996 law—a clause that everyone agrees is very poorly drafted, and that Congress may revise or even repeal. Ask your adviser for an update.

Briefly, here's the background: Medicaid is the only government program that covers the cost of nursing home care—but you aren't eligible for Medicaid until you've exhausted most of your own assets. In the past few years, people who expect to need nursing home care increasingly have transferred their assets to their children. The most common strategy is to give away your house, but keep a life estate—i.e., lifetime occupancy rights.

It's important to do this 'Medicaid planning' before you need nursing home care, because when Medicaid looks at your assets to determine your eligibility for financial help, it includes anything you transferred to someone else within three years of your application.

You're not permanently disqualified from receiving Medicaid even if you have given away assets. Let's say you gave away a house worth $125,000. Medicaid divides that $125,000 by the average monthly cost of nursing home care in your area—say $5,000. The result is 25—and that means you're ineligible for Medicaid for 25 months.

But the clock starts ticking the day the assets are transferred, not on the day of your Medicaid application. In other words, if you transferred the house and applied for Medicaid two years later, you'd be eligible in one month.

Here's the snag: The 1996 law appears to make some Medicaid planning asset transfers a felony, punishable by a fine or jail time or both. I say "appears" because the law's wording is open to conflicting interpretations. Some lawyers say it criminalizes most Medicaid planning. Others say it doesn't. The consensus is that the government is extremely unlikely to prosecute anyone under this statute. ("Are they going to drag Grandma out of the nursing home into jail for this? I don't think so," says one attorney.)

Indeed, a statement by the U.S. attorney general has made it clear that careful Medicaid planning is still legal. There's now a move in Congress to repeal this section of the 1996 law.

**NOTE:** When you give your house to your children but keep a life estate, for tax purposes it's exactly as if you left them the house in your will. The value of the house is included in your estate when you die. And because you kept lifetime occupancy rights, your kids will receive the house at its market value when you die. That means they can then sell it without incurring a taxable gain *(see **Q11**)*.

## Q11 What about putting my house into a qualified personal residence trust?

This strategy is worth considering only if you have a substantial estate tax to worry about.

Let's say you have a $500,000 house. You put it into a personal residence trust for 10 years, with your children as the trust beneficiaries. If you die before the trust expires, the house is still yours—and its full value is still in your estate. If you survive the 10-year term, your children own the house; and if you continue living there, you're legally required to pay fair market rent.

Not surprisingly, most people recoil at the thought of having to negotiate a lease to live in their own house. "This is something to consider doing with a vacation house, not with a primary residence," says Alan Weiner, senior tax partner at Holtz Rubenstein in Melville, New York.

You can discount the value of the gift because your kids had to wait 10 years to get it. The discount is based on a government table that changes every month. In November 1996, for example, a $500,000 house in a 10-year trust would have been discounted 40 percent, so you'd pay gift tax on only $300,000. You also avoid the estate tax on all the future appreciation of the house; who knows, its market value may be $800,000 by the time you die.

The longer the term of the trust, the bigger the discount in the value of the house—but the less chance you have of outliving the trust, too. And if you don't outlive it, you haven't reduced your estate tax.

**NOTE:** A major drawback to this arrangement is that your kids receive the house during your lifetime. When they sell it, they'll owe taxes on all its appreciation above your original purchase price. If you bought it for $100,000 and they sell it for $500,000, they'll have a $400,000 taxable gain. If they inherited the house at your death instead, they'd get it at its fair market value on the day you died. If it was worth $800,000 at that point, they could sell it for $800,000 without owing any taxes on the money.

## Q12 Do I need a power of attorney?

Yes. *See "Marriage and Divorce,"* **Q7**.

## Q13 Do I need a living will or a health care proxy?

Yes. *See "Marriage and Divorce,"* **Q6**.

## Q14 What can I do to provide for a disabled child?

You need to make financial arrangements for the child's future that avoid jeopardizing any government assistance he or she is entitled to receive.

The vehicle most often used is a 'special needs' trust, which holds money for the child's needs. You can name yourself and your spouse as trustees and make the trust a beneficiary of your will. One way to fund it is with a second-to-die life insurance policy. This one policy covers both of you less expensively than two policies, and pays only on the second death *(see "Insurance,"* **Q14***)*.

The wording of the trust document is critical. If it suggests the trust is your child's primary source of support, the income it throws off can eliminate or reduce his or her Supplemental Security Income benefits. SSI, which is funded by federal and state taxes, pays benefits to people of any age who are blind or disabled as well as to low-income people who are over 65. The government can demand reimbursement for these benefits from any assets or income owned or received by SSI beneficiaries.

The trust document should specifically say that the income it pays isn't to be used for the child's food, clothing, or shelter, for example. SSI pays for those necessities. The trust income must be used only to supplement SSI—by paying for a special educational need, for example, or to hire a companion. And this income can't be paid directly to the child;

it must pay the service providers.

There are other trusts that can be funded with a child's own assets—an inheritance, for example, or the proceeds of a personal injury case—without jeopardizing his or her eligibility for Medicaid and other government programs, says Robert Freedman, a partner at Freedman & Fish in New York City.

You need a lawyer who has expertise in these trusts—some of which are used for elderly beneficiaries as well as disabled children—and who is also familiar with your state's laws. The National Academy of Elder Law Attorneys in Tucson (at 520-881-4005) can refer you to someone in your area. Other good sources of information are the National Alliance for the Mentally Ill or NAMI (800-950-6264), or The Arc, formerly the Association for Retarded Citizens (800-433-5255). Both associations have local chapters nationwide and keep lists of attorneys who specialize in disabled children's needs.

**NOTE:** An alternative to creating your own trust is to join a communal or master trust, like those run by NAMI or The Arc. A communal trust is shared by many families, each of which has its own account within the trust just as each individual investor has his or her own account in a mutual fund. "A communal trust is very helpful if you don't have family members or close friends willing to take on the responsibility of acting as trustees for your own trust," says Freedman.

## Q15 What can I do to provide both for my second spouse and the children of my first marriage?

The traditional answer is a qualifying terminable interest property trust—less formally known as a Qtip trust.

This trust can provide income to your surviving second spouse for life; then the principal can go to the children of your first marriage.

**NOTE:** Ask whether your state law gives your surviving spouse the option to claim a portion of your estate outright instead of receiving lifetime income from a Qtip trust. That right can be waived in either a prenuptial or a postnuptial agreement.

**NOTE:** Don't set up a Qtip trust without considering the respective ages of all your heirs. If your second spouse is close in age to your adult children, for example, the children are likely to wait a long time for their stepparent's death. You may want to make provision for them to receive part of that inheritance at your own death instead of waiting to inherit the principal of a Qtip trust.

CHAPTER

# Losing
## YOUR JOB

HERE'S NOTHING DISGRACEFUL or unusual about losing your job. In fact, in today's economy it's a common experience. It's been estimated that workers graduating from college in the 1990s will change jobs seven or eight times in the course of their careers, not always by their own choice. According to the Department of Labor, 8.4 million Americans were pushed out of their jobs involuntarily from 1993 through 1995 alone. These layoffs happened at a time when the U.S. economy was humming along at a slow but steady pace that produced record corporate profits and stock market results—and they happened at some of the nation's largest companies.

In other words, sudden unemployment can and does happen to the best people and at what otherwise seem to be the best of times.

If you're being downsized or pushed into early

retirement by a big company, there's probably a personnel or human resources manager who can tell you your options with regard to severance pay, retirement savings and pension plans, and the health and life insurance benefits provided by your soon-to-be-former employer.

But even if you're lucky enough to have good sources of information and assistance within the company, you should also double-check what your employer tells you with your own financial advisers. Many of the rules that affect your options must comply with federal and state tax laws. Your tax accountant probably knows more about these laws than the corporate human resources staff—and he or she definitely knows more about your personal financial situation. You need to know the potential consequences of the choices available to you.

## Q1 What steps should I take ahead of time if I have reason to expect I'll be laid off?

Pay down your debt, maximize your access to new cash, and find out all you can about your severance and employee benefits options should your expectations materialize. If you've tossed or lost all those employee benefits brochures, this is a good time to ask for new copies.

It's also a good idea to tell your boss why your name shouldn't be added to the list of expendable employees, says Alan Johnson, a New York City employee benefits and compensation consultant. "I'd walk in and say, 'Since downsizing is in the air, I want you to know my special circumstances.' Remind him that you've done a great job, that you're in the middle of a special project, that the company just moved you here from across the country six months ago, that your wife just got laid off, that you have small children and a huge mortgage." Even if you don't avoid being fired, you will have laid the groundwork for getting a better severance package *(see Q2)*.

Other important steps:

◆ **Pay off your credit card balances.** If your credit card debt costs 18 percent interest, paying it off has the same effect on your wallet as if you had invested in a totally safe bond that earns 18 percent a year—tax-free. Start with the card that charges the highest interest rate, not the one with the biggest balance.

To replace your cards with less expensive ones, send $5 to RAM Research for a copy of CardTrak, a monthly report that lists the lowest-cost credit cards nationwide. Every issue includes low-rate cards and no-fee cards. (To order, send a $5 check to RAM Research at P.O. Box 1700, Frederick, MD 21702.)

◆ **Establish a home equity line of credit while you're still employed**; banks aren't crazy about lending to jobless people.

Many lenders now impose inactivity fees on lines that aren't used. "It might cost you $100 or more a year," says Keith Gumbinger, an analyst at HSH Associates, a mortgage research firm in Butler, New Jersey. "But that could be a cheap insurance policy if you fear you're going to be laid off." Don't use the credit line until you lose the job.

◆ **Fatten your paycheck by reducing or even stopping your contributions to the company 410(k) plan**—but don't spend the money. Use it to pay off high cost debt or if you have none, deposit the extra income in a money market fund or a bank savings account.

◆ **Don't take out a 401(k) loan without first finding out what would happen to it if you lost your job.** You should ask about this in any event, if you already have an outstanding 401(k) loan.

Most 401(k) loans must be repaid within five years. But if you leave the job, you typically get only 60 days to repay the outstanding balance before the loan is treated like an early withdrawal. If that happens, you'll have a whopping tax bill the next April 15th. On a $10,000 loan, federal and state income taxes, plus the 10 percent early withdrawal penalty (assuming you're under 59 and a half) can easily add up to $5,000 or more.

But ask what your company's rules are. Some 401(k) plans will give you up to six months to repay an outstanding loan. And a few companies actually let terminated employees maintain their 401(k) loan repayment schedule as if they were still employed. (You can also now roll a 401(k) loan into a new employer's 401(k) plan—assuming that its rules allow the transfer.)

## Q2 Can I negotiate a severance package?

You certainly have nothing to lose by trying. Focus on preserving as many of your employee benefits as possible.

For severance pay, the rule of thumb is one week's salary for one year's service. It's not unknown for companies to provide two or three times that much to higher-paid employees, however—or to everyone, in a very big layoff.

Even if you can't get the company to pay you more, you may be able to negotiate whether your severance is paid in a lump sum or as a continuation of your salary for a specified amount of time after you leave the job. In general, financial advisers recommend the lump sum, because you can immediately invest it in a bank or money market account to earn interest. But find out whether continuation of salary would include continuation of your employee benefits; if so, it's a better deal than a lump sum payment.

**NOTE:** If you take a lump sum in the last half of the year, talk to your tax adviser about whether you should ask to receive it in two installments—one now, and one next January—so that taxes on it will be spread over two years. This makes sense if you'll be in a lower tax bracket next year; it doesn't make sense, however, if your tax bracket will probably be the same—especially if you've already paid the maximum Social Security tax for this year.

**NOTE:** If you take the continued salary, ask your tax accountant if it makes sense to have your former employer reduce your tax withholding in the severance payments, too.

Ask your employer whether your group life and group disability coverage are convertible to individual policies. "When you leave the job, you're supposed to get a conversion notice on group life within 30 days," says Barry Barnett, a principal at benefits consultant Kwasha Lipton Group of Coopers & Lybrand, LLP, in Fort Lee, New Jersey. "But most employers forget."

**NOTE:** Comparison shop for life and disability insurance. You may find cheaper coverage elsewhere *(see "Insurance,"* **Q3** *and* **Q15**, *and "Epilogue")*.

Ask your employer what happens to your medical flexible spending account, if you have one *(see "Marriage and Divorce,"* **Q3***)*.

Briefly, you can contribute up to $2,000 or $3,000 a year to this flexible account through payroll deduction, and must use or lose the money within the year. Some companies let you draw out the entire amount early in the year. "You can submit an eligible medical bill for $2,000 in January and get paid for it," says Barnett. "But if you lose your job in February, the company may take a big hit out of your last paycheck to cover the advance. You should be prepared for it."

Other things to ask for, although you may not get them: Open-ended outplacement support; use of a desk and telephone while you look for another job; cash for vacation time not taken; accelerated vesting in your retirement plans; employer-paid health benefits until your severance expires, or depending on your age, until you're 65 and qualify for Medicare. And by all means, try to negotiate an arrangement to do part-time or consulting work as an independent contractor for your former employer.

"Always ask," says Alan Johnson. "You'd be amazed at the number of people who don't." Remember, you're no longer an employee; you're a vendor negotiating a deal.

## Q3 What should I do with my 401(k) plan balance?

It depends on your age, your financial situation, and the plan's rules.

Legally, you're now entitled to leave your money in the 401(k) plan after you leave the job, no matter what the reason, if you have $5,000 or more in your account. If you decide to do that, as a plan participant you must be treated the same way as active workers. Whether or not it's an attractive option depends partly the plan's investment choices, but even more importantly on its distribution rules.

**NOTE:** It's vital to find out how easily and how soon you can tap your money if it stays in the 401(k) plan.

◆ **Will staying in the plan give you penalty-free access to your money before you turn 59 and a half**? By federal law, you avoid the 10 percent early withdrawal penalty on money taken from a 401(k) plan if you're 55 or older when you leave the job. You may want to consider leaving your money in the plan, however, depending on its rules. Some companies won't let you take 401(k) withdrawals until you're 65. If that's the case in your plan, you're better off rolling it into an IRA, where you can start tapping it free of penalty when you turn 59 and a half. (If you're over 55 but under 59 and a half, consider taking some cash to live on before rolling your 401(k) balance into an IRA.)

◆ **If you have an outstanding 401(k) loan, can you continue repaying it on schedule by remaining a plan participant**? If so, keeping your money in the plan could let you dodge an imminent income tax liability (*see* **Q1**).

If you decide to roll your money into an IRA, make sure it goes into a new rollover IRA. Don't add it to your existing IRA. Keeping this money in a rollover IRA preserves your option to roll it into another employer's 401(k) plan at some future date.

*Do not have a check for your 401(k) balance made out to you and then deposit it in the rollover IRA.* Ask your employer to do a direct, trustee-to-trustee transfer and have the money deposited directly into your new IRA account. Here's why: Any check made out to you will be for only 80 percent of your money; 20 percent will be withheld for taxes— just in case you don't open that IRA.

If your 401(k) account is worth $100,000, for example, you'll get a check for $80,000. If within 60 days, you deposit $100,000 in an IRA, the $20,000 that was withheld will be refunded to you by the next April or May, says Ed Slott, a Rockville Centre, New York, tax accountant and author of *Your Tax Questions Answered.*

But in the meantime you face a classic Catch-22, unless you happen to have a spare $20,000 lying around to add to your IRA deposit. "The IRS says, 'Your 401(k) was worth $100,000. You deposited only $80,000 in an IRA. You owe income tax on the $20,000 that's missing—plus a 10 percent penalty if you're under 59 and a half,'" says Slott. And what happens? Instead of getting a $20,000 refund, you get back $20,000 minus income taxes and penalty.

## Q4 What should I do with the company stock in my 401(k) and/or profit-sharing plan?

This decision can make a big financial difference to you.

Most employers give you the option of rolling their stock out of your retirement plans into an IRA either as shares or as cash. It's usually better to take the stock, says Russ Kelley, a financial planner at Ayco, in Albany, New York, because that way you can control when you sell shares.

But the big question is whether to transfer this stock to an IRA, or into a taxable account instead.

If you transfer your company stock to an IRA, you preserve its tax-deferred status. You can sell the shares without tax consequences and diversify into other investments. That's what you should do if this one company's stock now accounts for the lion's share of your retirement portfolio.

But if not, you may be better off transferring the stock into a taxable account instead. If you do that, you will owe income taxes, plus a 10 percent penalty if you're under 55—but when the stock is part of a lump sum 401(k) distribution, the tax applies *only on the value of the shares at the time they were added to your account, not on their current market value,* says David Foster, a financial planner at Foster & Motley in Cincinnati (see Section 402 of the Internal Revenue Code).

That can save you a bundle if your stock has greatly appreciated in value since it first went into your 401(k) account. The tax on all the appreciation isn't due until you sell the shares—and at that point, you'll owe long-term capital gains tax on it, now capped at 20 percent. By contrast, in an IRA the appreciation is all eventually subject to ordinary income taxes, which currently go as high as 39.6 percent.

There's even a bonus for your heirs: if the stock is in a taxable account, at your death they'll owe taxes only on the increase in its value *before* you took it out of your 401(k) plan. If the stock were in an IRA, its entire value would be taxable to them. The main downside to transferring stock from a 401(k) plan to a taxable account: The dividends will be annually taxable.

But consider carefully whether or not you actually want to own this stock. "That's more important than any tax issue," says Foster. *(For more on your retirement account choices when leaving a job, see "Retirement," Q5.)*

## Q5 What are my health insurance options when I leave the company?

If you're not covered under a spouse's group health plan, find out the deadline for extending your current coverage under COBRA after you leave your job—and don't miss it.

Under the federal Consolidated Omnibus Reconciliation Act, better known as COBRA, you're entitled to buy coverage in your former employer's health insurance plan after you leave the job. It's not inexpensive. You pay the full cost of the insurance, plus a 2 percent administrative fee—but you'll almost certainly get more benefits than you can purchase elsewhere. Any company that employs 20 people or more must offer COBRA coverage to workers who leave.

You and your dependents are entitled to COBRA benefits for 18 months. If you're disabled within 60 days of termination, says Kwasha Lipton's Group's Barnett, you can buy another 11 months of coverage for 150 percent of the usual premium. (At that point, as a disabled person, you qualify for Medicare.)

After your COBRA benefits expire, you must be given the right to convert from the group coverage to an individual policy without passing a physical—if your group plan has a conversion option. Many plans don't. Generally, if the health coverage is provided by a third party, there's a conversion clause, says Barnett; if you're covered by your employer's self-insured plan, there isn't.

If your company offers both an indemnity health plan and a health maintenance organization plan *(see "Marriage and Divorce," Q4)*, chances are that one of them has a conversion option and the other doesn't. "Don't throw away the literature on your former employer's open enrollment period," says Barnett. "Your COBRA rights give you the same privilege as current employees to change your plan during the open enrollment. If the HMO provides a conversion option and the indemnity plan doesn't, use the enrollment to switch to the HMO."

If you can't convert COBRA coverage to an individual policy, you'll have the unenviable task of shopping the market for health insurance. Your likeliest options:

◆ **Blue Cross/Blue Shield**. Most of the Blues are not-for-profit organizations; in some states, they must take all applicants. (This can make their coverage mighty expensive.)

A major medical policy from the Blues usually pays 80 percent of doctors' and hospitals' fees, diagnostic tests, and prescription drugs above an annual deductible. Routine checkups and preventive care usually aren't covered. The policies typically have annual and lifetime caps on the total dollar amount of benefits they'll pay.

◆ **A local HMO that lets individuals join**. In an HMO, you'll pay a preset monthly fee and small co-payments for each visit to a doctor or hospital, but they must be in the plan's approved network. There's no deductible and preventive care is covered. Usually, there's no coverage for prescription drugs.

Questions to ask when shopping for health coverage:

◆ **What percentage of medical expenses is reimbursed, and what's the annual cap on my out-of-pocket costs?**

◆ **How many hospital days a year are covered?**

◆ **What's the lifetime benefit limit?** Many policies have $1 million or $2 million lifetime caps, but some are lower. You may be able to buy a higher cap for additional premium.

◆ **What are the policy exclusions?**

◆ **What are the rules on preexisting conditions?** Some policies don't cover anything diagnosed in the six months before you bought coverage; others go back three years.

Are you wondering what happened to the much ballyhooed, bipartisan Health Insurance Portability Act of 1996? It was signed into law, all right. But it provides much less than the self-congratulations of President Clinton and Republican Congressional leaders would lead you to think. The new law merely guarantees that if you had group coverage in your old job, you can't be denied coverage in a new job regardless of your medical history. You still may need COBRA to cover the three- to six-month waiting period many employers impose before a new employee is eligible for health insurance.

The new law doesn't help you if you had no health insurance in your old job—or if you leave a job where you had coverage to become self-employed.

## Q6 How should I adjust my household budget while I'm unemployed?

You need a basic cash flow analysis to figure out how long your existing funds will carry you.

Your sources of income are your spouse's paycheck, interest on savings and investments—excluding your tax-deferred retirement accounts—and unemployment insurance. You may qualify for it even if technically you resigned and got severance. (In some states, you're eligible for unemployment insurance if you lost a job because your spouse was transferred to another city.)

The amount of unemployment insurance you'll receive varies from state to state; it's based on a percentage of your wages, up to a dollar maximum—usually less than $300 per week. How long you can collect benefits also depends on the state; typically, they last for 26 weeks. Admittedly, that's not much, and it is taxable income. Consultants say people often pass it up. That's foolish. You're entitled to this money, and it will come in handy.

Your cash reserves are your lump sum severance, bank accounts, and any investments you own, again excluding retirement accounts. Potential sources of low-cost money include a home equity loan *(see "Your House,"* **Q11***)*; a loan from a cash value insurance policy *(see "Insurance,"* **Q3** *and* **Q9**); and any after-tax contributions you made to your 401(k) plan.

When you leave the job, your employer will cut you a separate check for after-tax 401(k) contributions, because they're not eligible for an IRA rollover. This money is tax-free because you've already paid taxes on it. (The interest it earned is taxable, however, and should be rolled into an IRA along with the rest of your 401(k) balance.)

Cut your living expenses to the bone while you're out of work. You must make mortgage or rent payments and cover the cost of utilities, food, insurance, and gasoline. Try to put everything else on hold.

Send in the minimum monthly payment on your credit card bills. Write to the day-care center, the orthodontist, and all your other creditors, explaining your situation and asking them to agree to partial payment or a temporary suspension of payments until you find a job. Even your mortgage lender may be amenable to giving you more time if your past credit history is good. Banks don't like to foreclose if they can avoid it.

If you're heavily in debt, call the National Foundation for Consumer Credit, a nonprofit organization with member offices nationwide (800-388-2277). They can help you negotiate a repayment schedule with your creditors. The service is confidential and the cost is very low.

Reduce the expenses you can't eliminate. If you have an older car, drop your collision insurance, for example. Stop eating out and buying take-out food and scale down the birthday and Christmas gifts. But don't overdo it or you won't be upbeat enough for job interviews. You should feel that you're coping resourcefully with a temporary crisis—not hammered into the ground by unemployment.

**NOTE:** Keep a record of your job hunting expenses—travel to interviews, long distance calls, the cost of printing and mailing résumés, career counseling, etc. They're tax-deductible if you itemize your deductions, to the extent that they exceed 2 percent of your adjusted gross income limit. In other words, if your income was $50,000, you can't deduct the first $1,000 of expenses. You don't have to find a job to qualify for the deduction, but you do have to be looking for a job in your current line of work. The government won't subsidize career changes (a rule that seems outdated in the economy of the 1990s). (See IRS publication 529, *Miscellaneous Deductions*. To order, call 800-829-3676).

If you relocate to take a new job—even in a new career—you can deduct your moving expenses. But the rules are very specific: these expenses are deductible only if you work at the new job for at least 39 weeks of the first year after the move, and if that job is 50 miles or more farther from your house than your old job was—and only to the extent that the cost of the move wasn't reimbursed by your new employer. (See IRS publications 529, *Miscellaneous Deductions,* and 521, *Moving Expenses*).

Don't touch your retirement accounts until you've exhausted all other sources and negotiated every possible extension with creditors. IRAs, 401(k)s, Keoghs, and other tax-deferred accounts are exorbitantly expensive money; the taxes can eat up 50 percent of every dollar you withdraw.

As a last resort, tap these accounts only for the immediate need—one mortgage payment at a time, for example. You owe taxes and early withdrawal penalties only on the amount you withdraw.

**NOTE:** If you have access to a 457 plan (a deferred compensation plan for state and municipal employees), that's the one to tap first. It's not a qualified retirement plan, so there's no early withdrawal penalty, although withdrawals are taxable.

**NOTE:** You can avoid the 10 percent penalty on IRA withdrawals before age 59 and a half if you take a series of substantially equal payments based on your life expectancy, and continue taking them for at least five years or until you reach age 59 and a half, whichever is longer. Then you can stop if you want to.

This works well if you're in your early fifties and have a substantial amount in your IRA. Let's say you're 53 years old and have a $500,000 IRA. The IRS actuarial table gives you a 30.4-year life expectancy; so you can withdraw $16,447.36 a year for six and a half years, owing taxes on the money, but no early withdrawal penalty.

This equal payments route (which accountants call 'annuitizing') isn't such a good deal if you have only $50,000 in your IRA and are only 35 years old: Your life expectancy is 47.3 years. You're entitled to take out just $1,057 a year penalty free, and must keep doing it for 24 and a half years. (See IRS publication 590, *Individual Retirement Arrangements.*)

### Q7 Should I change my investments?

There's no reason to reinvest your retirement savings, but consider replacing some of your taxable equity investments with a short-to-intermediate bond fund, or laddered Treasuries, or CDs to produce an income stream.

If you decide to do this, sell any depreciated securities first. You can use up to $3,000 a year of capital losses to offset any kind of income, says Ed Slott. You should also look back to see if you had any losses in past years that you couldn't deduct then, but could carry forward to use now. If you had $5,000 of losses last year, for example, you could only deduct $3,000, but the $2,000 balance can be used this year. "Unused losses are carried forward indefinitely until used up," Slott says. "They expire only when you die. Your estate can't use them."

CHAPTER

7

Taxes

THE SIMPLEST AND SUREST way to reduce your taxes is to earn less. This is apparently the only method of tax avoidance with no popular appeal. There are people willing to try everything else. The promise of tax-deferral or tax-exemption probably sells more investments than any other sales pitch.

Financial advisers unanimously counsel against investing in anything only, or even chiefly, for tax reasons. And anyway, few investment tax shelters survived the tax reform of 1986. But that doesn't mean there's no wiggle room left.

On the contrary: Tax law is full of gray areas whose meaning is legitimately open to interpretation. You can be a conservative or aggressive interpreter of the law, and you should let your tax adviser know which approach you prefer. This is strictly a question of your comfort level. Aggressively interpreting the law to your advantage is perfectly legal and doesn't automatically mean you'll be audited; by the same token, a conservative approach doesn't guarantee that you won't be audited.

But don't think you can fudge indisputable facts, like your marital status, or whether or not you participate in a pension plan at work—and avoid any adviser who suggests that you do. This happens. Shortly after my husband and I married, our then-tax accountant told us that tying the knot was a poor financial decision since our tax bill would be lower if we weren't married. "But never mind," he added, cheerfully. "We'll just pretend you didn't tell me you got married last year and you can file as single people." We quickly sought another tax accountant.

Remember that taxes impact your financial life

throughout the year. Take the time to find out the tax consequences of major decisions like starting a business, getting married or divorced, taking a buy-out from your job, and more mundane ones like buying or selling investments—before you act on them.

And of course, tax laws change. As this book goes to press, the 1997 tax law is just days old. Among its major new provisions:

◆ A cut in the maximum capital gains tax rate from 28 percent to 20 percent.

◆ A tax exclusion on up to $500,000 of your profit when you sell a primary residence if you're married filing jointly, and $250,000 for single taxpayers. This exclusion will replace both the tax deferral on profit rolled into the purchase of another primary residence of equal or greater value within two years of the sale, and the one-time tax exclusion on up to $125,000 of profit if you're 55 or older and selling the house you've lived in for three of the past five years.

◆ An increase in the income limits that qualify for tax-deductible contributions to Individual Retirement Accounts. Under the new law, over the next eight years a $2,000 annual IRA contribution will gradually become fully tax-deductible for single taxpayers earning up to $50,000, and over the next 10 years, it will become fully deductible for married couples earning up to $80,000.

◆ A new IRA, called the Roth IRA. Contributions, limited to $2,000 a year, aren't tax-deductible; but if you don't tap the account for five years, its earnings are tax-free when used to buy a first home or pay college expenses. They're also tax-free if you've held the account five years and you're at least 59 and a half years old. Eligibility for these new Roth IRA accounts phases out for single taxpayers earning from $95,000 to $110,000 and for married couples earning $150,000 to $160,000.

◆ A new education IRA. Families who meet income

requirements—earning up to $150,000 for couples and up to $95,000 for single taxpayers—can contribute $500 a year per child. Contributions aren't tax-deductible, but earnings used to pay for education are tax-free.

## Q1 What's my marginal tax rate?

This is important information for any investor—even someone who never ventures into the stock market.

If you and your spouse have $98,000 a year in combined income, you may think that you're in the 31 percent federal tax bracket. The reality is more complex: you pay a 31 percent federal income tax only on the last $1,100 you earn. In fact, your *marginal* tax rate is 31 percent, but most of your income is taxed at 15 percent or 28 percent.

For a married couple filing jointly in 1996, the 28 percent federal rate kicked in for amounts over $40,100; the 31 percent tax rate applied to amounts over $96,900; the 36 percent rate applied to amounts over $147,700; and 39.6 percent was levied on amounts over $263,750. (Federal tax brackets are adjusted at the end of each year for inflation.)

Perhaps that last $1,100 of your $98,000 income is investment income that you don't currently need. If so, you might reduce your marginal tax rate to 28 percent by switching from that income-paying investment into a growth investment that generates minimal dividend income, like an equity index fund. You wouldn't owe taxes on the increase in the value of your index fund shares until you sold them—at which point, if you'd held the fund for a year or more, you'd owe a long-term capital gains tax, now capped at 20 percent.

Or if you want to stay invested for income, you might consider a tax-exempt municipal bond fund instead of a taxable corporate bond fund.

On the other hand, if your marginal tax rate is low, investing in tax-exempt municipal bonds doesn't really make sense for you. If your marginal tax rate is 31 percent, earning 5 percent interest tax-free is like earning 7.25 percent in a taxable investment. If your marginal rate is only 15 percent, a tax-free 5 percent is worth only as much to you as 5.88 percent in a taxable investment. You might earn more in Treasuries, which are free of state and local taxes—and safer than municipal bonds.

## Q2 Am I taking advantage of all the tax breaks available to me?

This is always worth asking.

The best way to reduce your taxes is to make the maximum possible contributions to your retirement plans, because those contributions reduce your taxable income. This is true of contributions to qualified retirement plans (401(k) plans, IRAs, Keoghs, SEP-IRAs, 403(b) plans) and to deferred-compensation plans like 457s.

But there are others:

Are you taking full advantage of any flexible spending accounts your employer may provide for child-care expenses or medical expenses that aren't covered by insurance? Contributions to these accounts also reduce your taxable income, dollar for dollar. You can set aside up to $5,000 a year for child care or elder care expenses; your contributions to a medical care FSA are typically limited to $2,000 or $3,000 a year *(see "Marriage and Divorce,"* **Q4***.)*

Have you considered giving away highly appreciated investments? Let's say you own 100 shares of stock for which you originally paid $10 a share; the stock is now worth $35 a share, or $3,500. Your capital gain is $2,500. If you give the stock to a charity, you'll avoid the tax on this profit and at the same time you'll be able to claim a charitable tax deduction for the full $3,500. (*Note:* Charitable contributions of appreciated assets are limited to 30 percent of your adjusted gross income.)

You could make the same gift to your children or grandchildren whose capital gains tax rate is lower than yours. (Under the new tax law, long-term capital gains are taxed at 10 percent for taxpayers whose marginal tax rate is 15 percent, and at 20 percent for taxpayers whose marginal tax rate is higher.)

For example, you could give highly appreciated stock to your college-bound son or daughter, who could sell it, pay a lower tax than you would, and use the money for tuition. There are no tax consequences to you if the total value of your gift to each child is no greater than $10,000 in any tax year.

Gifts also reduce potential estate taxes. Grandparents can make unlimited gifts to cover their grandchildren's college expenses (or anyone else's, for that matter), provided the check is made out directly to the college, says Ed Slott, a Rockville Centre, New York, tax accountant and author of *Your Tax Questions Answered.* The unlimited exclusion applies only to tuition and not to books, supplies, dormitory fees, board, or other items that aren't direct tuition costs. This is a wonderful way to reduce estate taxes, he adds, especially if the recipient is the ultimate heir of the estate anyway.

Other tax deductions are much less appealing:

◆ **Unreimbursed medical expenses** are deductible only if they exceed 7.5 percent of your adjusted gross income. (See IRS brochure 502, *Medical and Dental Expenses.*)

◆ **Casualty and theft losses not covered by insurance** are deductible only if the loss exceeds 10 percent of your adjusted gross income. And the first $100 of each loss isn't tax deductible. (See IRS publication 547, *Casualties, Disasters, and Thefts.*)

◆ Miscellaneous expenses, like the costs associated with investing (such as fees to financial planners), tax preparation, or looking for a job are deductible only if they exceed 2 percent of your adjusted gross income. (See IRS publication 529, *Miscellaneous Deductions.*)

(IRS publications can be ordered by calling 800-829-3676. *For a list of other useful IRS publications, see "Appendix."*)

**NOTE:** A potentially large but obscure deduction that isn't subject to this 2 percent limit is available to some beneficiaries of Individual Retirement Accounts, notes Slott. Let's say you inherit an IRA from your father. You'll owe income taxes on this money as you withdraw it from the account. But if your father's estate was taxable, you're entitled to an income tax deduction for the amount of federal estate tax attributable to the IRA.

**Q3** **How much can I claim in charitable deductions for all the clothing and household items I gave away last year?**

Much less than you hope.

The IRS doesn't value property you give away as generously as you do. "People pay $600 for a suit and want to claim $200 when they give it away," says Theodore Harris, a New York City tax lawyer. "The IRS allows what the Salvation Army can sell it for—maybe $15."

You're entitled to claim only the fair market value of donated goods at the time of the donation. For gifts worth under $250, you must have a receipt from the charity describing the gift. If you value your gift at more than $500, you must also attach IRS Form 8283 to your return, explaining how you arrived at your valuation. If you claim the donation is worth more than $5,000, you must include a written appraisal from a qualified appraiser. (See IRS publications 526 and 561, *Charitable Contributions,* and *Determining the Value of Donated Property.*)

**NOTE:** Churches and synagogues automatically qualify as legitimate charities. If you're in any doubt about the tax status of other charitable organizations, you could look them up in IRS Publication 78, *Cumulative List of Organizations,* a huge, two-volume list that's available at many public libraries. Or call the IRS at 800-829-1040 and ask. They'll tell you. Ask if contributions are tax-deductible, too. "An organization may be on the list because it has tax-exempt status, but that doesn't necessarily mean donations to it are tax-exempt," says Robert Kobel, an IRS spokesman.

**Q4 What taxes must I file for my babysitter/ nanny/housekeeper?**

You'll be sorry you asked, even though you need this information.

When you employ anyone 18 years old or older in your home, or anyone to whom you pay more than $1,000 a year, regardless of their age, you must withhold from their wages appropriate amounts for Social Security and Medicare taxes (better known as FICA), Federal Unemployment tax (FUTA)—and in most states, state unemployment tax, too.

You'll find instructions on how to do all this in IRS publication 926, *Household Employer's Tax Guide.*

You withhold 7.65 percent of the employee's salary for FICA. You'll send this money to the government— along with your share of FICA, which is also 7.65 percent of the employee's salary. Can you generously pay both your share and the employee's share? Yes—but if you do, your payment of her share is considered additional wages on which she owes income taxes. (The extra payment doesn't increase her wages for FICA taxes, however.)

You're not legally required to withhold money for the employee's federal and state income taxes, but you must do so if she requests it. In fact, you should consider doing it even if she doesn't ask you to, unless you're sure she'll set aside enough money to pay income taxes on April 15—not an easy task, especially for someone on a modest salary.

And then there's the paperwork.

When you hire a household employee, you must apply for an employer identification number and have the employee fill out W-4 forms. Every year, you file a W-2 form for her with the Social Security Administration along with Form W-3. Until recently, you also had to file quarterly tax forms to both the federal government and the state. State forms are still a quarterly requirement, but the federal government mercifully has replaced most of them with a new Schedule H, which is part of your own annual income tax return.

**NOTE:** The federal taxes for household employees are due by April 15, even if you get an extension for your own taxes.

Complying with all these requirements takes time and can embroil you in a bureaucratic maze: When I employed a full-time babysitter, the federal government gave me not one but two employer identification numbers—and then sent increasingly ominous letters demanding to know why one of me wasn't filing quarterly forms and taxes. Six months' worth of letters and telephone calls in reply failed to correct the error. I finally went in person to the local IRS office, where the second ID number was deleted from the computer. (Meanwhile, New York State classified me as a small manufacturer for reasons I never figured out. For the next couple of years, the state sent me workers compensation notices to post in my factory.)

## Q5 What's the best way to handle a tax deduction the IRS may challenge?

Attach a note to your return explaining it.

If you're claiming an unusually big deductible expense in relation to your total income, for example, you can often head off an audit by attaching extra information to your tax return. "If you had $20,000 of medical expenses, my advice would be to attach copies of the doctors' and hospital's bills to your return, and write 'See receipts attached' where you take the deduction," says Alan Weiner, senior tax partner at Holtz Rubenstein in Melville, New York.

The IRS computer may flag your return because of the unusually large deduction. But if that happens, it will be examined by an IRS agent who'll see the receipts and may process the return without further question.

The computer automatically checks the relationship between income and deductions, so it's a good idea to explain anything unusual. "If you suffered a big casualty loss, note the date and explain the nature of the damages. And if the President has declared your town a federal disaster area, say so," advises Ed Slott. "Or if your deductions are the same as last year's, but your income is much smaller because you were laid off for part of the year, explain that."

If you know you're taking a potentially controversial deduction, it's also a good idea to attach a note to your return indicating that you know it, says Weiner.

"There are cases where the rules are unclear and there's a large amount of tax involved," he explains. "For example, there's a section of the Internal Revenue Code saying you can't deduct losses associated with a hobby. But maybe your losses meet the test as business losses."

If you just go ahead and take this deduction and it's later challenged and rejected by the IRS, you'll owe additional taxes and interest, plus a penalty equal to 20 percent of your underpayment. If you take the deduction and attach a form disclosing that you're taking a controversial position, it increases the likelihood you'll be audited. But even if that happens, and the IRS successfully challenges the deduction, you'll owe only the extra tax and interest—not the 20 percent penalty.

**NOTE:** The IRS takes a dim view of tax returns claiming deductions that defy common sense. The 20 percent penalty may also be applied to a substantial tax underpayment that results from a deduction, credit, or exclusion that any reasonable person should have known was "too good to be true," unless you can show you took steps to verify that your claim was correct. A 'substantial underpayment' is $5,000 or 10 percent of the correct tax, whichever is greater.

## Q6 What triggers a notice from the IRS?

Careless mistakes and discrepancies.

All tax returns are scanned by a computer that immediately picks up basic mistakes like errors in math, entries that don't square with those on your W-2 or 1099 forms, or missing Social Security numbers and W-2 forms. While these mistakes by themselves won't necessarily trigger an IRS audit, they will result in IRS notices asking for additional information or documentation or explanation for a discrepancy.

Among the common errors that are sure to be flagged:

◆ Forgetting to report interest and dividend income or capital gains. Bank and brokers report these payments to the IRS, and the information is no longer on flimsy little 1099 slips. It's on computer tape. (See IRS publication 550, *Investment Income and Expenses.)*

◆ Forgetting that state retirement income is federally taxable, even if it's exempt from state taxes. (See IRS publication 525, *Taxable and Nontaxable Income.)*

◆ Incorrectly calculating your capital gains tax The tax is levied on your profit—the sale price minus your original cost. When you sell a stock that pays tax-free dividends, your cost is reduced by any tax-free dividends you've received. When you sell mutual fund shares, all your reinvested dividends are added to your cost. (See IRS publication 551, *Basis of Assets.)*

◆ Forgetting municipal bond income that makes part of your Social Security benefits taxable. The IRS gets reports from municipal bond funds. (See IRS publication 564, *Mutual Fund Distributions.)*

◆ Failing to report pension distributions that you rolled into an IRA, or interest from municipal bonds— even though these aren't taxable events or income.
When a bank or mutual fund transfers money out of one of your tax-deferred accounts, it reports the transaction to the IRS. If you don't volunteer that you rolled the money into another tax-deferred account, the IRS assumes that you took a taxable distribution. As for municipal bonds, the IRS wants you to report the tax-free interest, because it wants to keep track of who owns municipal bonds. (Apparently, these bonds have a mysterious way of disappearing from people's estates when they die.)

◆ Overestimating or failing to document your charitable contributions. (See IRS publications 526 and 561, *Charitable Contributions* and *Determining the Value of Donated Property.)*

**NOTE:** Don't assume when you get an IRS notice that the IRS is right and you're wrong. The IRS isn't infallible. In fact, a 1988 audit by the General Accounting Office found the IRS made mistakes in nearly one-third of its notices.

The notice may be a request for information you already provided. Or it maybe be based on misinformation from other sources. For example, banks sometimes mistakenly report IRA interest to the IRS, even though it's not taxable. A couple of years later, the taxpayer is likely to get an IRS notice saying he failed to report interest income from this bank account.

After a brief panic attack—the normal reaction to an IRS notice—the taxpayer calms down, figures out which bank account the notice refers to, turns his files inside out, locates the documents showing this is an IRA account and that therefore the interest isn't taxable, makes copies of everything and sends them to the IRS. His relief is short-lived. In response, the IRS sends a second notice demanding the tax, interest, and penalty.

But there's nothing to worry about. The second notice merely means that the new information hasn't yet been entered in the IRS computer. Until it is, the computer automatically sends another notice every 30 days. (How do you know the IRS has received and accepted your reply? You stop getting notices, that's how.)

You can minimize the agony of this correspondence by sending everything certified mail, return receipt requested. It's also a good idea to put a daytime and evening telephone number on all letters to the IRS, and to file the change of address form (Form 8822) whenever you move, says Alan Weiner. If you don't, IRS notices about your 1995 return will be mailed to your 1995 address—even if you've filed tax returns from a new address for the past two years.

## Q7 What triggers a tax audit?

Major discrepancies between your return and the typical tax return for people in your income bracket.

The IRS computer's Discriminate Function program, or DIF, screens every tax return. It's designed to
detect anything that falls outside the parameters of a
normal American tax return. If your income was
$25,000 and you claimed $10,000 in charitable contributions, DIF flags your return. If you have a $200,000
income and you live in an expensive zip code, but you
don't claim a deduction for real estate taxes, DIF flags
your return. If you claim a mortgage interest deduction
that's substantially higher than the average for people
in your income bracket, the computer spots you.

When the computer kicks out your return, it's
examined by an IRS agent. If there are documents
attached to it explaining the aberration to the agent's
satisfaction, the return may be processed without further delay. On the other hand, the higher your DIF
score, the likelier it is that the return will be audited.

Some items are particularly likely to result in an
audit. Among them:

◆ Unreported income. The computer compares the
income you report on your return with the income that
has been reported by everyone who pays you money.
Your wages are reported to the IRS on W-2 forms;
everything else is reported on 1099 forms—your
income from interest, dividends, real estate rentals,
retirement plan distributions, rental income, lottery
and gambling winnings, sales of stocks and bonds, tax
refunds, and even from the sale of your home.

◆ Exemptions and child-care credits you claimed for
fictitious dependents. More than seven million dependents vanished from tax returns after it became a
legal requirement to list your dependents' first and

last names and Social Security numbers, notes tax accountant Ed Slott. "But people still list children who no longer live with them, or who never existed in the first place.

The IRS also pays attention to how many dependents you've claimed. "A couple with $15,000 in income who list 12 dependents will most likely be hearing from Uncle Sam, just to check up on the family," says Slott. (See IRS publications 501 and 503, *Exemptions, Standard Deductions, and Filing Information,* and *Child and Dependent Care Expenses.*)

## Q8  How should I handle an audit?

Calmly. Don't be nervous, don't be flustered, don't be scared—be prepared.

When the IRS announces you're being audited, it also states specifically what the audit is about. Take time to read the audit announcement letter carefully—it will be awhile before your eyes focus—and concentrate on gathering and organizing all the pertinent information. If the audit appointment is inconvenient, or you need more time to prepare, do not hesitate to ask that it be rescheduled.

Don't panic if you don't have documentation for every deduction you've taken. The IRS does accept oral explanations, reconstructed records (clearly identified as such), and approximations, within reason. Of course, the better prepared you are, the better the audit will go. The auditor is likelier to allow a few missing receipts if the records you do have are neat, detailed, and filed in chronological order.

You can give a tax professional your power of attorney to represent you at the audit, or go by yourself. You can also accompany your tax accountant—but financial advisers unanimously counsel against that option. If you tag along, you're paying for professional help, but are just as vulnerable as if you went in by yourself because you could ruin everything by blurting out the wrong information. (Merely saying, "Gee, I've always taken that deduction," for example, could expand the audit to include previous years' returns.)

A tax professional has the benefit of experience, can negotiate on your behalf more skillfully than you can for yourself, and in your absence can always say, "I don't know the answer to that question, I'll have to get back to you." It isn't as believable if you say you're ignorant about your own finances.

If you decide to represent yourself, bring only the information the IRS asked for—nothing else. Don't mention anything unrelated to the subject of the IRS letter you received. The agent doing an audit isn't supposed to ask about anything else, explains IRS spokesman Robert Kobel. But if you *volunteer* unrelated information, it immediately becomes a legitimate subject for the agent to pursue.

The average taxpayer's worst mistake during an audit is to dissipate his or her nervousness by making small talk. New York City tax attorney Theodore Harris remembers one client so relieved when his audit was over that he became conversational and told the IRS agent about his son's rabbinical studies scholarship. "A scholarship?" replied the agent. "I think that constitutes additional income to you."

The five best answers to an auditor's questions are Yes; No; I don't recall; I'll have to check on that; and What specific items do you want to see?, according to tax lawyer Frederick W. Daily, author of *Stand Up to the IRS* (Nolo Press)—must reading for anyone going into a tax audit alone. Daily also suggests you prepare by getting and reading IRS publication 1, *Your Rights as a Taxpayer.*

If you feel the auditor isn't treating you fairly, or

you want to appeal his or her interpretation of the tax code, don't hesitate to ask to see a supervisor.

## Q9 What are my options if I can't pay my tax bill?

File Form 9465 to ask the IRS for an installment payment plan—but file your tax return on time.

If you pay your tax late, the penalty is half of one percent per month (plus interest, of course.) But if you file your tax return late, you owe an *additional* penalty equal to 5 percent a month on the balance you owe, up to a maximum of 25 percent.

The IRS will tell you within 30 days after you file your request to pay in installments whether it has accepted it. (If you can show severe financial hardship, file Form 1127 and you may be granted up to a six-month extension.) But in any event, you'll still owe interest on the late payments. The interest rate charged by the IRS is a little over the prime rate.

**C H A P T E R**

8

# Retirement

ETIREMENT IS *THE* investment goal of our time, and a major theme of virtually all financial product marketing. You do need to save for your retirement. But don't accept at face value what so many "educational" marketing campaigns keep telling you—that you must save enough money during your working years to generate 70 percent to 80 percent of your preretirement income during the 20 to 30 years you'll spend in retirement.

To save that big a nest egg, most people would have to live on cat food during their working years.

Fortunately, there's no reason to assume you can't live comfortably on less than 80 percent of your preretirement income, especially if you work part-time after you're officially retired—and you may discover that work is as necessary to your psychic well-being as it is to your financial health.

Two or three decades is an awfully long time to live without the emotional rewards and the daily structure of a job.

Looking at their parents' experience has given baby boomers a distorted perspective on retirement. A well-funded, work-free retirement is a historical aberration unique to the generation that reached adulthood in the 1940s and 1950s and were lucky enough to enjoy generous employer-paid pensions, great appreciation in real estate values thanks to inflationary and demographic trends, and an expanding Social Security system. Earlier generations had no such concept of retirement—nor will future generations.

It's impossible to generalize about how much money you'll need to live comfortably in retirement. Ask a tax accountant or a fee-only financial planner for an objective assessment of how much income you'll need based on the specifics of where and how you want to live. Bear in mind, too, that your expenses are likely to change, perhaps substantially, during your retirement years. Two or three decades is a long time. You may spend a lot on travel during the first third of your retirement, become a provident homebody during the middle years, and spend lavishly on medical care in the last years.

You should also consult a tax adviser about your choices with regard to withdrawals from your Individual Retirement Accounts. The rules governing IRA withdrawals are horrendously complex and can have significant financial consequences—and they depend largely on irrevocable decisions that you must make when you turn 70 and a half.

Today, you may think of an IRA as a relatively small account that you funded with annual contributions of $2,000 or less. But by the time you retire, most of your money will be invested in IRAs. They'll contain everything you roll over from your 401(k) and other retirement plan balances when you leave your job.

## Q1 How much money will I need to live comfortably in retirement?

If ever a question called for a custom-tailored answer, this is it. The answer depends on variables, some of which are specific to you and all of which can only be estimated—your living expenses, your life expectancy, and the rate of inflation during your retirement.

You could go nuts trying to factor these variables into a retirement budget on a pocket calculator. Fortunately, you don't have to. A financial adviser with good computer software can do a cash flow analysis of your retirement expenses under different scenarios—

and a series of calculations to figure out whether your portfolio is invested to generate the income you'll need *(see* **Q13***)*.

A fee-only planner or tax accountant will charge you a flat fee or an hourly rate capped at a specific maximum for this kind of analysis. You should expect to pay from $800 to $1,500. An adviser who earns commissions for selling investments may charge less for the service, or even do it for nothing—but his analysis may serve his needs better than yours.

Whoever crunches the numbers for you, you'll have to supply the data to feed into the computer. The more complete your information and the better organized it is, the more accurate the results will be, the less work the adviser will have to do, and the less the analysis will cost you. It may take some research to come up with the information you'll need, especially if you plan to move after you retire *(see* **Q2** *and* **Q3***)*.

Start with your current household budget, listing all your expenses—housing, utilities, food, gasoline, insurance premiums, entertainment, and taxes. Go through a couple of years' worth of canceled checks and credit card statements to make sure you've included everything.

Then go back and slowly eliminate or modify everything that will or may change. Cross out work-related expenses and the cost of the mortgage and the children's tuitions if they'll be paid off by the time you retire. You can eliminate disability insurance after you no longer have a salary to protect; maybe you can drop life insurance, too, if your children are grown and your savings are big enough to take care of a surviving spouse.

But you should expect to spend more than you do now on travel and entertainment—and on health insurance. Very few employers provide health coverage for their retirees, and Medicare typically covers less than half of the average senior citizen's health care bills. You can count on Medicare for basic coverage for hospital stays above an annual deductible; it also pays 80 percent of most doctor and laboratory costs. But it doesn't cover prescription drugs, preventive care like annual physicals and flu shots, hearing aids or eyeglasses, or (with very limited exceptions) the cost of nursing home or home health care.

**NOTE:** You can get more information about Medicare, and advice about buying supplemental private coverage (called Medigap), from a free federal counseling program provided in every state under the auspices of the federal Health Care Financing Administration. Don't forgo this advice. The cost of Medigap varies widely and you can easily buy more than you really need if you don't know what you're doing. For more information, call your local department on aging. (For free copies of *Your Medicare Handbook* and the *Guide to Health Insurance for People with Medicare,* call the Social Security Administration at 800-772-1213.)

A good retirement budget must also factor in your life expectancy; tell your financial adviser if you come from an unusually short- or long-lived family. Most people are startled at how many years they'll live based on the IRS actuarial table—as unsentimental a forecaster of longevity as you could hope to find. (See IRS publication 590, *Individual Retirement Arrangements;* to order, call the IRS at 800-829-3676.) Most financial planners today run projected annual cash flow calculations for healthy retirees up to age 90 or 95.

## Q2 Should I move?

This decision involves many financial and emotional considerations, from the local cost of living, taxes, climate, and crime rate, to your proximity to family and friends and access to good medical care, entertainment, and transportation.

Selling your house can substantially increase your investable cash in retirement: Profit from the sale of a house you've owned and lived in for two of the last five years is tax-free up to $500,000 for married couples filing jointly, and up to $250,000 for single taxpayers. This can be a meaningful opportunity, especially if your house represents the lion's share of your assets. In that case, selling it will give you the money to diversify into other investments that provide more liquidity, growth, and income than a house.

Selling your house may also enable you to move into a smaller house or apartment that's easier and less expensive to maintain—perhaps in a part of the country with a better climate and lower taxes.

First identify the places you'd consider moving to; then find out what it actually costs to live there. The public library is an excellent source of magazines that regularly rate the best places in the country to live, and books about picking a good place to retire. To find out more about any community you're seriously considering, write to the local chamber of commerce, take out a three-month subscription to the local newspaper, and spend a couple of vacations there.

**NOTE:** Two very important factors people often forget when choosing a place to retire are the availability of public transportation and the availability of part-time work.

You may be attracted now to a serene rural community with low taxes, but its proximity to a town will be important to your ability to get part-time work if you need or want it. And although getting behind the wheel of a car may be second nature today, you may find that's no longer true, especially after dark, when you're in your late seventies or eighties. Think carefully before moving to a community where your independence depends heavily on your willingness and ability to drive.

If the proceeds from selling your house add up to the lion's share of your assets, don't be too quick to buy another one. It may make more sense to rent, if buying would cost 50 percent or more of your investable money. Remember, a house is a single illiquid asset that doesn't throw off income—and may not appreciate in value.

"What if the neighborhood goes downhill? What if an interstate highway is built next door?" says Ray Russolillo, director of personal financial services at Price Waterhouse in New York City. "You can't afford those risks unless you also have a decent-sized financial portfolio." Even if your house does grow in value, he points out, you won't be able to realize its appreciation as easily as you can cash in the growth of a mutual fund investment.

## Q3  Should I pay off my mortgage?

As you near retirement, revisit the pros and cons of prepaying your mortgage and establishing a home equity line of credit *(see "Your House," **Q10** and **Q11**).*

Paying off your mortgage can substantially reduce your living expenses in retirement; on the other hand, you might earn more by investing elsewhere.

Your return on the money you use to pay off your mortgage is whatever the mortgage costs you. If the mortgage costs 8 percent a year, that's your return on your money when you pay it off. Compare it with what you'd earn in other safe investments—a money market or short-term bond fund if you're likely to need the money in less than five years, or a conservative stock fund for longer than five years.

You should also consider diversification: If the

house is your only asset, your money is better invested elsewhere than in paying the mortgage. (And if your mortgage rate is substantially higher than what you'd earn elsewhere, you can almost certainly refinance it for less.)

If you do pay off your mortgage, preserve your access to your investment in the house by opening a home equity line of credit a few years before you retire.

Age won't prevent your getting a home equity loan after you've retired; it's illegal for lenders to discriminate on the basis of age. But you will have to meet income and credit requirements, even if your equity in the house is more than enough to cover the amount you borrow. That might be easier while you still have a salary.

## Q4 Can I retire early?

Fat chance.

Judging by the letters I get from readers, a great many people want to retire at 55 or even younger. This is a wildly unrealistic goal for most people.

Anyone who retires at 55 needs a nest egg big enough to support him or her for a long, long time. At 55, you have a life expectancy of 28.6 years according to the IRS unisex actuarial table. (You're likely to live somewhat longer if you're a woman, not as long if you're a man.) The IRS uses median numbers: the average person of either sex has a 50 percent chance of living longer. In fact, financial advisers typically suggest that you add five years to your life expectancy as it appears on the IRS table, in order to cut the risk that you'll outlive your money down to 15 to 20 percent.

You can be sure the cost of living will increase during those 30 years or so of retirement. If you retire on $30,000 this year and inflation averages just 4 percent a year, in a decade you'll need $44,000 to pay the same bills; in 28 years, you'll need $90,000 a year.

At 55, you're not old enough to collect Social Security. And taking early retirement will substantially reduce the Social Security benefit you eventually receive—an amount based partly on the number of years you worked and the age at which you begin getting benefits. The earliest you can receive Social Security benefits is age 62; and then, you receive only 80 percent of the amount you'd get if you waited until age 65. If you were born after 1959, you'll get only 70 percent of your total benefit at age 62.

You're ineligible for Medicare until you turn 65. So you'll have to buy private health insurance for 10 years—a substantial expense, even for a healthy 55-year-old.

Finally, you're too young at age 55 to take withdrawals from your Individual Retirement Accounts without incurring a 10 percent early withdrawal penalty as well as ordinary income taxes *(see* **Q5** *and "Losing Your Job,"* **Q3***)*.

Delaying your retirement pays off on three levels: the later you retire, the more time you have to save money for retirement, the more time your savings have to grow, and the less time your investment earnings will have to support you.

### Q5 Which pension plan/401(k) plan payout option should I take?

You need a financial adviser to explain how each potential choice would affect your personal financial situation.

Among your likely options:

◆ Taking a lump sum payment from your 401(k) and other defined contribution plans and rolling the money into an IRA. This has several clear advantages. In an IRA, you have unlimited investment choices and tax-free transfers from one investment to another; you're free to take withdrawals or not as you wish until after you turn 70 and a half; you pay income taxes only on the amounts you withdraw.

If this is your choice, make sure you do a direct, trustee-to-trustee transfer from your 401(k) plan to the IRA *(see "Losing Your Job,"* **Q3**. *Also see "Losing Your Job,"* **Q4**, *for your distribution choices for any company stock you own in your retirement plan)*.

**NOTE:** Bear in mind that if you're 55 or older when you leave your job, you can take money out of your 401(k) without incurring the 10 percent early withdrawal penalty. In an IRA, that penalty applies until you're 59 and a half. "One mistake I see older people make is rolling their money into an IRA without first taking advantage of the opportunity to avoid the 10 percent penalty by taking out cash they need to live on," says David Foster, a financial planner at Foster & Motley in Cincinnati.

◆ Taking a lump sum, immediately paying taxes on it, reinvesting the money in taxable accounts. This can make sense if you're eligible for favorable tax treatment known as five-year or 10-year averaging: you pay taxes on your lump-sum distribution as if you had spread the withdrawals over the next five or 10 years. The effect is often to drop you into a lower tax bracket—sometimes to cut your tax rate on this money in half.

The government gives you a lower rate in exchange for collecting taxes on the entire amount upfront. To qualify, you must take the entire balance of *all* your defined contribution plans in a single tax year. (The terms 'five-year' and '10-year' averaging are mislead-ing: the tax may be lower, but it is all due in the year the lump sum is paid.) Under current tax law, if you're at least 59 and a half and were born before 1936, you may choose either five-year averaging or 10-year averaging for taxes on eligible lump sum retire-ment payments. People born after 1935 can use only the five-year averaging method—and as of 2000, five-year averaging will no longer be available.

But five- or 10-year averaging has a major draw-back: Your money is no longer in a tax-deferred retirement account. Your future investment earnings will be taxable.

**NOTE:** Payouts from 403(b) plans and 457 plans aren't eli-gible for five- and 10-year averaging—and 457s aren't eligi-ble for IRA rollovers, either. But most 457 plans give you the right to leave your money growing tax-deferred in the plan until you turn 70 and a half, if you wish.

◆ Leaving your money in a 401(k) plan. This is your legal right if your balance is $5,000 or more. It may be an attractive option when you retire, if the plan offers good investments and good service and you're reluc-tant to tackle investing on your own in an IRA.

But check your employer's rules on 401(k) plan dis-tributions to retirees. You need access to this money after you retire. Some plans let you take money out in installments over a 10- or 15-year period. Others only let you take the entire balance in a single, lump sum payment. No 401(k) plans currently offer the total withdrawal flexibility you'd get in an IRA.

If you're lucky enough to have a traditional pension too, you may get a choice between taking it as a life-time annuity or as a single, lump sum payment.

Which makes more sense? It depends partly on how the lump sum is calculated. Ask your employer what interest rate assumption the lump sum is based on and discuss the answer with your financial adviser. (If the interest rate assumption is 6 percent, for example, that tells you that you'd have to average a higher return than 6 percent on the lump sum for the rest of your life to improve on the monthly income the annuity pays.)

It also depends on what other retirement assets you have. An annuity gives you the security of monthly income. The federal Pension Benefit Guaranty Corp. insures most pension plans that pay a monthly benefit. Assuming yours is one of them, you can rely on at least a portion of that income even if your former employer goes bankrupt.

The downside is that a fixed annuity payment won't keep pace with inflation.

If you have other assets invested for growth, you might choose an annuity as the most conservative piece of a diversified retirement portfolio. But if this money represents your main retirement asset, you're probably better off taking the lump sum, rolling it into an IRA, and investing in diversified mutual funds for growth as well as income.

**NOTE:** Don't buy a variable annuity—an annuity that offers a choice of mutual fund investments —without reading about its drawbacks in "Investing," **Q13**.

## Q6 Should I take a single life pension annuity or a joint and survivor pension annuity?

Almost always, you should take the joint and survivor pension.

If you're married, many traditional pension plans give you a choice between a monthly benefit for your lifetime only and a monthly benefit that is smaller, but lasts for two lifetimes—yours and your spouse's. If the single life benefit is $28,000 a year, the joint benefit might be $21,000 a year, for example.

Life insurance agents often suggest that you take the bigger single life benefit, and then use the extra income to buy a life insurance policy. The idea is that when you die, your surviving spouse can use the policy proceeds to buy an annuity for income to replace your terminated pension benefit.

This idea is called pension maximization, or pension max.

Pension max sounds great—but it works only if:

**1** The single life pension pays you more income— *after taxes and after paying the insurance premium*— than you'd have received from the joint and survivor pension; *and*

**2** After you die, the insurance policy will pay enough to buy your surviving spouse an annuity income at least equal to what the joint and survivor pension would have paid.

Pension max very rarely meets both tests.

**NOTE:** Don't opt for pension max without first getting an after-tax comparison of your choices from a financial adviser who has no stake in your decision.

Pension max may work for you if you're younger and healthier than most retirees. In that case, you might be able to buy insurance more cheaply outside your pension plan, because it charges all retirees the same rate for the joint and survivor benefit without regard to their age and health. You should also consider pension max if you're a woman and the pension plan uses unisex rates; again, your insurance cost outside the plan might be lower.

But for most people, actuaries say the potential dangers of pension max seriously outweigh the benefits.

Among the risks:

◆ **You won't buy a big enough life insurance policy to protect your spouse.** The after-tax difference between a single life pension benefit and a joint and survivor benefit is rarely big enough to buy an insurance policy that will adequately cover the spouse, says James Hunt, an actuary and a director of the Consumer Federation of America Insurance Group. (Remember, the policy premium must cover the agent's commission and the insurer's overhead and profit, as well as the death benefit.)

To find out how big an insurance policy you'd need to replace a survivor benefit, Hunt says, you should multiply that benefit by 12 if your pension isn't indexed for inflation—and by 15 or more if the pension is indexed for inflation. To replace a $21,000 annual survivor benefit in a pension that's not indexed, he estimates you'd need a $250,000 life insurance policy. At age 65, your premium for that policy might be twice as much as the annual after-tax income you gain by taking the single life benefit.

◆ **Interest rates will fall, driving up the cost of your policy.** Pension max typically uses interest-sensitive policies to reduce the cost of coverage, says Hunt. The premiums are based on rosy assumptions about future interest rates. But those assumptions aren't guaranteed. If the insurer's investment return doesn't live up to its expectations, you may have to pay a higher premium to maintain the policy or accept a smaller death benefit.

The premium for a pension max policy must be big enough to fund that policy for your lifetime even if interest rates fall. If the policy illustration assumes the insurer will earn more than 6.5 percent, says Hunt, the premium isn't high enough to protect you adequately from interest rate risk.

◆ **Your future expenses will be higher than you think.** If for any reason you can't afford to maintain the coverage until you die, your surviving spouse will be unprotected.

◆ **Interest rates will be lower when you die than when you bought the policy**. If that happens, the policy death benefit won't buy your surviving spouse as big an annuity as you expected.

By federal law, you can't opt for a single benefit from a private pension plan unless your spouse formally waives the right to the joint and survivor pension. Any spouse should think long and hard before doing so, says Larry Elkin, a financial planner in Hastings-on-Hudson, New York: When you waive your entitlement to that survivor benefit, he notes, who gets the larger pension check? Your spouse does. And who owns the life insurance policy that protects you? Your spouse does. If the marriage ends, what assurance is there that he or she will maintain the policy or keep an ex-wife or ex-husband as the beneficiary?

## Q7 How much will I get from Social Security?

It depends on the number of years you paid Social Security taxes, the amount you earned, the age at which you begin collecting benefits, and the year in which you retire.

Call or visit your local Social Security Administration office before deciding when to apply for benefits. The agency staff is very patient about explaining all your options—and there's no charge.

Over the long term, a monthly Social Security check on average replaces 42 percent of a worker's monthly preretirement salary; lower-paid workers get a higher proportion, and higher-wage earners get less. The average retired worker today collects $745 per month—a little more for men, and a little less for women. The maximum benefit for a person who retired at 65 in January 1997 is $1,326 per month.

If you're married, when you turn 65 you're entitled to a benefit equal to half of your spouse's benefit; and as a widow or widower at 65, you're entitled to a benefit equal to 100 percent of whatever your spouse was getting. (If you want to collect these spousal benefits when you're younger, you'll get smaller amounts.) In other words, if your benefit is $600 a month, for example, at age 65 you and your spouse together are entitled to collect $900 a month; at your death, if your surviving spouse is at least 65, he or she would collect $600 a month. These rules apply for both men and women.

**NOTE:** Anyone who is entitled both to a Social Security benefit based on his or her own earnings and to a spousal benefit gets the greater of the two —not both. This is something to discuss with a Social Security representative. "Sometimes it makes sense to take one benefit early and then switch at age 65 to the other. For example, you could take an early spousal benefit in a reduced amount, and then at age 65 switch to the full amount of the benefit based on your own earnings," says John Clark, a Social Security spokesman.

You can start taking benefits at 62; but the amount will be permanently lower if you start collecting a benefit before you reach full retirement age. For people born before 1938, that's age 65; for those born after 1943, it's age 66; and people born after 1959 aren't eligible for their full retirement benefit until age 67. It can make sense to delay taking benefits: the amount you're entitled to receive will increase by a certain percentage for each year you wait to start collecting benefits up to age 70.

**NOTE:** Don't decide when to start collecting Social Security without finding out how your age affects the size of the monthly benefit.

Social Security benefits are adjusted annually to keep pace with inflation—a plus not available in most private pensions. In fact, today's Social Security beneficiaries don't merely receive back what they paid in—they get a lot more:

A person who retired at age 65 in 1979 after paying the maximum Social Security taxes all his or her working life recovered those taxes in less than two years. People with average earnings who retire at 65 today will get back the taxes they paid (plus interest) in about six and a half years—and remember, the average 65-year-old collects Social Security for about 15 years if he's a man, and about 20 years if she's a woman.

Future retirees won't get as sweet a deal. But although Congress will modify future benefit increases, you can bet it won't renege on the basic promise. Social Security may not amount to a lot, but it *will* be there for you.

At any age, you can find out roughly how much to expect by calling Social Security at 800-772-1213 and asking for Form SSA-7004. After you complete and return the form, the Social Security Administration will send you a copy of your earnings history, plus its estimate of the amount you'll collect in retirement based on that history and your own estimate of your future earnings.

It's a good idea to do this every two or three years, if only to correct any clerical errors in the record. "I once discovered by filing this form that Social Security had inadvertently missed one year of my earnings," says Alan Weiner, senior tax partner at Holtz Rubenstein in Melville, New York.

## Q8 Whom should I name as my IRA beneficiary?

This decision will affect your IRA withdrawals during your lifetime, as well as how the IRA is taxed when you die.

Naturally, you should name an IRA beneficiary when you open an IRA, no matter how old you are. (And you can change the beneficiary anytime you wish.) But your choice becomes crucially important after April 1 of the year after you turn 70 and a half, which is when you're required to start taking money out of your IRA. (If you turned 70 and a half in 1997, for example, your deadline would be April 1, 1998. *See* **Q11**.)

Your beneficiary choice as of this deadline determines how long you can stretch out your mandatory annual IRA withdrawals. Here's why:

Your minimum required withdrawal every year is determined by your life expectancy as it appears on the IRS actuarial table. (See IRS publication 590, *Individual Retirement Arrangements*.) The shorter that life expectancy, the bigger your minimum annual withdrawal, and the faster you have to empty the IRA. (You can always take out more than the required minimum, of course.) It's to your advantage to keep mandatory withdrawals as small as possible because money that stays in the IRA keeps earning tax-deferred income.

You can use either your single life expectancy or your joint life expectancy with your beneficiary to determine the mandatory withdrawals. The joint life expectancy will be longer—and the required withdrawals therefore smaller.

You can change your IRA beneficiary at any time, as often as you wish, as long as you live. *But you can't change your minimum distribution schedule. It's locked*

*into your joint life expectancy with the beneficiary you
named on the April 1 deadline.*

Let's say that you named your spouse, with whom
you have a 10-year joint life expectancy. Then, after
you turn 70 and a half, your spouse dies and you
remarry a much younger person, with whom you
have a 40-year life expectancy. You can make your
new spouse your IRA beneficiary—but your withdrawal schedule will still be based on the 10-year life
expectancy.

**NOTE:** If you calculate your joint life expectancy with a nonspouse beneficiary—your child or your grandchild, for example—you must assume for the purposes of the calculation
that he or she is only 10 years younger than you are.

**NOTE:** Consider estate taxes when naming an IRA beneficiary, says Alan Weiner: If you name your spouse, there
won't be any estate taxes on the IRA at your death because
there's an unlimited estate tax exemption on assets left to
a spouse. If you leave the IRA to the kids, its value over
$600,000 will be subject to federal estate tax; and smaller
amounts may be subject to state estate taxes depending on
where you live.

**NOTE:** Don't fail to name a beneficiary. If no one is designated, your estate becomes your IRA beneficiary by default.
"Your estate has no life expectancy, so income taxes could
immediately be due on everything in the IRA," says Rockville
Centre, New York, tax accountant Ed Slott.

## Q9 What IRA payment method should I pick?

It depends on how healthy and wealthy you are.

The minimum annual amount you must withdraw
from your IRA after you turn 70 and a half is deter-

mined partly by your choice of beneficiary *(see* **Q8***)* and partly by which of two payment methods you select.

The first method is to recalculate your life expectancy every year. The second method, called 'term certain,' is to calculate your life expectancy only once. You must choose which payment method you want to use by April 1 of the year after you turn 70 and a half—and the decision is irrevocable. If you don't specify what you want, you get the recalculation method by default.

Ask your financial adviser to help you figure out which method is better for you. They both have advantages and disadvantages.

With the recalculation method, you never have to empty your IRA because as long as you live, you have a life expectancy on which to base your minimum withdrawals. This may be important to you if you have a very large balance and want to prolong the tax deferral as long as possible.

But recalculation has a drawback, too: If you've been using a joint life expectancy with your named beneficiary and that person dies, your annual recalculations must be based on your single life expectancy. The effect can be that your mandatory IRA withdrawals suddenly accelerate.

Take a couple who are 72 and 68, for example. Their joint life expectancy is 20.8 years. Their minimum required withdrawal is the total balance of all their retirement accounts divided by 20.8. But if the 68-year-old dies, the next year's withdrawal for the survivor, now 73 years old, is based on his single life expectancy—13.9 years.

If you use the term certain method, you have to empty your IRA in a specific number of withdrawals. If the same couple use the term certain method, their IRA will be empty at the end of 20.8 years. The drawback if you use this calculation is that you may outlive the IRA. The advantage is that your withdrawal schedule won't be affected by your designated beneficiary's death.

The payment method choice also affects the treatment of your IRA after you die:

Let's say the 73-year-old names his kids as beneficiaries after the death of his spouse. If he uses the term certain method and dies before emptying his IRA, his children can continue taking withdrawals using the same schedule. If he uses the recalculation method, at his death the IRA balance immediately is paid out to his heirs, who must pay income taxes on it in a single tax year.

## Q10 How will my IRA distributions be taxed?

As ordinary income. The only exception is for money that was taxed before you put it into the IRA; your after-tax IRA contributions won't be taxed again.

You'll owe tax penalties in addition to ordinary income taxes, if you take any IRA distributions that are too early or too late, or too little. This rule applies to all qualified retirement accounts.

◆ Early withdrawals are those taken before you're 59 and a half years old. They're subject to a 10 percent penalty.

◆ Withdrawals that are late or too small are any mandatory distributions that you don't take after you turn 70 and a half years old *(see* **Q8** *)*.

There's a 50 percent excise tax on the difference between what you take out of your IRA and what you should have withdrawn. If your minimum mandatory annual distribution is $1,000, for example, and you withdraw nothing, the penalty is $500—and you owe it annually until you take the required withdrawal. You don't have to be a math whiz to see that this could quickly wipe out your IRA.

As noted above, you won't pay taxes on after-tax IRA contributions when you withdraw them. But that makes the withdrawals sound simpler than they really are. For tax purposes, your IRA accounts are a single pool of money. Adding after-tax contributions to the pool is like adding cream to a cup of coffee: You can't remove the cream separately. There's going to be a little bit in every sip you take.

**NOTE:** This rule will not apply to the new Roth IRA and Education IRA accounts created by the 1997 tax law (see "Taxes," page 176). These new accounts aren't considered part of the same pool of money as traditional IRAs.

To figure out the amount of tax-free cream in each IRA withdrawal, you have to add up your after-tax IRA contributions and calculate what proportion of the total IRA they represent. Let's say you put $10,000 into an IRA, of which $2,000 was in after-tax contributions. The IRA grows to $100,000. Your $2,000 nondeductible contribution represents only 2 percent of that $100,000—so only 2 percent of each withdrawal you take will be tax-free.

**NOTE:** Keep good records. You'll notice it's impossible to do this calculation unless you know your total after-tax contributions.

If your IRA beneficiary is your spouse, he or she can roll the balance into a new IRA of his or her own after you die. A nonspouse beneficiary can't roll the money into another IRA. But depending on the payment method and beneficiary selections you made during your lifetime, your nonspouse beneficiary may be able to choose between emptying your IRA over a five-year period or stretching the withdrawals over his or her own lifetime.

## Q11 When should I start taking IRA withdrawals?

It depends on your IRA balance, your life expectancy, and your tax situation, as well as on how much money you have in non-IRA accounts.

The deadline for taking mandatory IRA withdrawals is April 1 of the year after you turn 70 and a half. But you may be better off taking the first withdrawal in the year before this deadline. Here's why: If you turn 70 and a half in 1997, your deadline is April 1, 1998. Your deadline for the second mandatory withdrawal is December 31, 1998. In other words, if you wait until April 1 to take the first withdrawal, you'll wind up having to take two in the same tax year. That could be enough additional income to push you into a higher federal tax bracket and increase the tax on your Social Security benefit.

**NOTE:** Even if you take your first required IRA withdrawal by December 31 of the year you turn 70 and a half, you still have until the following April 1 to designate a beneficiary and choose a payment method *(see* **Q8** *and* **Q9***)*.

In general you should postpone tapping these accounts as long as you can afford to do so, to maximize their deferred growth.

## Q12 Should I change my investment mix when I retire?

Probably less than you think.

Many retirees think they can put their savings into fixed-income investments and live on the interest. Unfortunately, this strategy doesn't work unless you have so much money or such a short life expectancy that you don't have to worry about inflation.

Most retirees live well into their eighties. If you retire at 65, that means you may live to see the cost of living double or triple, even if inflation averages 4 percent a year or less. You must invest for growth as well as for income.

You may want to rebalance your portfolio to achieve a somewhat less aggressive mix, however. Without earned income, you're more vulnerable to the ups and downs of the stock market.

One way to insulate yourself from a potential bear market is to keep enough money in short-term investments to cover your expenses for five years, and invest the rest for growth. You could use money market or short-term bond funds for your income-producing investments, or buy Treasuries in staggered maturities *(see "Investing," Q7)*. You can maintain the five-year cushion by annually moving just enough money to cover one year's expenses from your growth investments into your income investments.

Obviously, it's crucial to know how much you'll need to cover a year's expenses—and this is a moving target. Your financial adviser's calculation must include a factor for annual inflation and interest rates.

**NOTE:** Don't be carried away by your desire to minimize taxes. Compare every tax-exempt investment with what you'd earn after taxes in a comparably safe or risky taxable investment *(see "Investing," Q12)*.

Even if tax-exempt municipal bonds would pay you more than taxable Treasuries, for example, they may not pay *enough* more to justify their market risk. And don't buy tax-exempt investments to avoid taxes on your Social Security benefit. It doesn't work *(see Q14)*.

## Q13 How much can I afford to withdraw annually from my investments?

The answer to this crucial question depends on how much money you have, and on three other factors that you must estimate: the investment return your money will earn, how long you'll live, and the rate of inflation.

A good financial adviser can crunch the numbers for you, illustrating how many years your money will last based on different interest rate and inflation assumptions and the size of your annual withdrawal.

Let's say you retire with $400,000, for example, and your money earns a 7 percent annual average return, while inflation averages 4 percent a year. If you withdraw $20,000 (5 percent of your nest egg) in your first year of retirement, and increase each annual withdrawal afterwards by 4 percent to keep up with inflation—taking out $20,800 in the second year, $21,632 in the third year, and so on—your money will last for 29 years.

Of course, if any one of these variables is changed, the answer changes, too. If you earn only 4 percent a year on your investments, for example, and all other things remain the same, your money will last 20 years. If you take out $40,000 in the first year, and all other things remain the same, your money will last 12 years. If you earn 8 percent a year on investments and all other things remain the same, your savings will last for 36 years.

Clearly, this calculation is an estimate that you'll want to revisit periodically as interest and inflation rates change. But it provides an essential blueprint for your retirement years—a blueprint that can help you avoid spending much more than you can afford, or investing far too conservatively to cover your expenses.

## Q14 How much of my Social Security benefit is taxable?

Up to 85 percent of it, depending on your other income—even if you don't work. And if you do work, you may forfeit $1 in Social Security benefits for every $2 or $3 you earn, depending on your age.

If you're single and have $25,000 to $34,000 in total retirement income, or married filing jointly with $32,000 to $44,000 in total income, up to 50 percent of your Social Security benefit is taxable. If you're single and have more than $34,000 in income or married with more than $44,000 in income, up to 85 percent of your Social Security benefit is taxable.

**NOTE:** Your total income for this calculation includes all tax-exempt income such as interest from municipal bonds, as well as half of your Social Security benefit.

This tax may be an important consideration for two people collecting Social Security and also contemplating marriage. Two single people can earn up to $50,000 a year in retirement income before their Social Security benefits become taxable. For married people, benefits are taxable when their income rises above $32,000.

Find out the impact of any wages you earn in retirement on your Social Security benefits. Working may not pay financially, even if it is emotionally rewarding.

In 1997, benefit recipients aged 62 to 64 must give back $1 in Social Security for every $2 they earn above $8,640. Benefit recipients between ages 65 and 69 have to give back $1 in benefits for every $3 they earn over $13,500. These caps are adjusted annually and disappear at age 70.

**NOTE:** You can temporarily stop receiving Social Security benefits if you choose, and begin collecting them again at a future point—with a recalculated retirement age that might allow you to collect a bigger benefit.

## Q15 Should I consider taking a reverse mortgage?

Maybe—if your house is your only asset, you don't want to move, and you don't qualify for a home equity loan. But a reverse mortgage is a last resort because it's an extremely expensive loan.

This is a loan for people 62 years old or older who want to tap the equity in their homes, but don't have the income to qualify for a regular home equity loan.

The amount you can borrow is based on your equity in the house, your age, and your life expectancy. You can receive the money in a lump sum, or in fixed monthly payments that last for a fixed term, like 10 years, or for as long as you live in the house. Or you can take the loan as a line of credit that you tap only as needed.

**NOTE:** This is one type of income that doesn't affect your Social Security benefits, because it's borrowed money.

Many lenders cap these mortgages at $207,000, which is the maximum loan they can sell to the Federal National Mortgage Association (Fannie Mae). The Federal Housing Administration offers reverse mortgages up to a $155,250 limit. Unlike Fannie Mae loans, the FHA mortgages must carry insurance, which adds to their cost. But the insurance guarantees you'll never owe the bank more than the value of your house. If you live there longer than expected and your loan is more than the house is worth, the insurance pays the difference.

**NOTE:** The amount of money you actually receive in a reverse mortgage is considerably less than the total amount of the loan. The interest likely to accrue on the loan is subtracted, as are the closing costs. The older you are and the lower the interest on the loan, the more money you get.

In a loan available on January 1, 1996, for example, a 65-year-old with $150,000 of equity in her house could take out $23,356 as a single lump sum of cash or as a credit line, says Ken Scholen, director of the National Center for Home Equity Conversion, a non-profit consumer association in Apple Valley, Minnesota. An 85-year-old with the same $150,000 of equity could borrow $64,432. (In both cases, the loan included $1,800 of closing costs, plus a $3,000 origination fee.)

Reverse mortgages are available in multiple forms. If you're a 75-year-old with a $100,000 debt-free house, you could take a reverse mortgage at 8 percent interest as $45,000 in a single cash lump sum; as a $45,000 credit line; as a $10,000 lump sum and a $35,000 credit line; or as monthly income of $360 for as long as you live in your house.

Comparison shopping is critically important. "No single reverse mortgage works best for everyone," says Scholen. "One plan may give you thousands of dollars more at a much lower cost than another plan."

The reverse mortgage isn't repaid until after you move or die. Then your house is sold and the lender recovers both principal and interest from the sale.

The big drawback of reverse mortgages is their cost, which includes steep fees. The origination fee, for example, isn't based on the amount you're borrowing, as it is in conventional mortgages, but on the assessed value of your house, which is always more than the loan. These and other closing costs, which you can borrow as part of the mortgage, typically are heavily loaded at its front end. It makes no sense at all to take a reverse mortgage if you're likely to sell the house in five years.

**NOTE:** Lenders by law must show you the total average annual cost of a reverse mortgage in writing. This makes it easier to comparison shop, which is essential. The cost of reverse mortgages can vary widely from one lender to another.

**NOTE:** Fannie Mae and FHA require that all reverse mortgage applicants receive counseling from an independent agency; many private lenders do, too.

For names of lenders making reverse mortgages in your area, and telephone numbers of counseling services in your area, call your local agency on aging or the Federal National Mortgage Association (800-732-6643), the Department of Housing and Urban Development (800-217-6980), or the National Center for Home Equity Conversion (612-953-4474).

# EPILOGUE

# Finding
# FINANCIAL
# ADVISERS

OU WOULDN'T CHOOSE a refrigerator, a car, or a college for your child without taking time to weigh the relative merits of several possibilities before deciding which one best fits your needs, preferences, and budget. Looking for financial advisers is no different: it will take research and comparison shopping on your part.

You need advisers who are smart, honest, and likable—and they're out there. With a little time and patience, and the resources listed in the following pages, you can find them.

A few basic rules to bear in mind, no matter what type of professional help you're looking for:

◆ Always ask what an adviser charges, what the fees are based on, and how much your specific job is likely to cost. There's nothing indelicate about these questions; no professional will blush to hear them.

◆ Expect to pay for expert advice. Consumers rightly resent paying commissions or fees that aren't disclosed or are revealed in such fine print that they're all but invisible; but they sometimes forget that the opposite of a hidden fee is a clearly disclosed fee—not free service.

◆ To make sure you don't overpay, determine the price range for the service you need by getting cost estimates from more than one adviser.

◆ Don't minimize the importance of finding an adviser who is congenial as well as expert in his or her field. There's no point in hiring someone you can't comfortably confide in.

◆ When you hire an adviser, ask for an engagement letter that spells out the services to be provided and what they will cost. This protects both of you. The letter should state that if it turns out the job will take longer and cost more than estimated, the adviser will call and tell you so before proceeding.

## FINANCIAL PLANNERS

 WHEN YOU LOOK FOR A DOCTOR, you can be reasonably sure all the candidates for the job meet a minimum standard of competence—four years at an accredited U.S. or Canadian medical school, one or more years of graduate medical education or residency, and a state license. With financial planners, there is no such established standard. Nationwide, there are about 250,000 people who describe themselves as financial planners. They range from sole practitioners to employees of local, regional, and national accounting firms, brokerages, and bank trust departments. Their educational and professional backgrounds and levels of expertise vary widely.

A financial planner's job is to help figure out where you stand financially, analyze your needs and goals, and create a practical strategy to meet them. This job doesn't necessarily include making specific investment recommendations, or buying or managing investments for you, although an increasing number of financial planners also act as portfolio managers. Fees to manage a portfolio of mutual funds range from 0.4 percent all the way up to 2 percent of assets.

**NOTE:** You can easily manage a no-load fund portfolio yourself, buying directly from the fund company. For the toll-free number of any fund company, call 800-555-1212, or check the annual mutual fund listings in *Forbes* and *Business Week*, or *Morningstar Mutual Funds*, all available at the public library. Morningstar also provides information about each mutual fund's objectives, historical performance, expenses, and investment strategy.

Because financial planners direct or influence the investment of hundreds of millions of dollars, they're intensely courted by financial services companies (including companies that sell no-load products). Your financial planner's objectivity depends largely on how he or she is compensated. You have four choices:

**1** Fee-only planners charge flat fees, hourly fees, and sometimes fees that are a percentage of assets under management. Hourly fees range from $75 to $250. Flat rates range from $1,000 to $4,000 or more, depending on the service and which part of the country you live in.

**2** Fee-based financial planners charge a combination of fees and commissions. They could as accurately be called commission-based planners. A fee-based planner might earn a fee for creating a financial plan, for example, and earn commissions from selling mutual funds and insurance to implement the plan. Fee-based planners typically earn most of their money from commissions. This means that they usually charge lower fees than fee-only planners; it also means that their product recommendations, while they may be good, are not disinterested.

**NOTE:** When you buy advice, it's essential that you stick with no-load or low-load products. If you don't, you're paying twice—once for the advice and again to buy the products you need. (There are other good reasons to stick with no-load products, too. *See "Investing,"* **Q4**).

**3** Fee-offset financial planners charge a flat fee from which they later subtract any commissions they earn from implementation of the plan. This seldom-used fee structure is designed to pay the planner the same amount, no matter what products you buy at his or her recommendation.

**4** Commission-only financial planners are paid on a transaction basis. This means they earn nothing unless you buy a product. The commission typically is a percentage of the price and is included in the price—i.e., you don't pay it separately; the larger it is, the more expensive the product is to you.

**NOTE:** You maximize your chances of getting disinterested advice by going to a fee-only financial planner. *But you should never turn your financial decisions over to any adviser, no matter how he or she is paid.*

Just because a financial planner's advice is objective doesn't mean it's also good. You need an adviser with expertise in areas as diverse as investments, taxes, insurance, and estate planning—and depending on your situation, you may want to find someone who specializes in a specific area, such as divorce, family businesses, or portfolio management.

The best general credentials to look for are:

◆ **Certified Financial Planner (CFP)**. This designation is issued by the Board of Standards and Practices for Certified Financial Planners in Denver. CFPs must pass a difficult 10-hour exam and agree to abide by a code of ethics. For referrals to CFPs in your area, call 800-282-7526.

◆ **Personal Finance Specialist (PFS)**. This designation is issued by the American Institute of CPAs. A PFS is a CPA with additional training in financial planning. To qualify, the adviser must pass an exam and have at least three years of professional experience in personal finance. For referrals to PFS planners in your area, call 800-862-4272.

Other resources:

◆ **The National Association of Personal Financial Advisors (NAPFA)**. NAPFA's 600 members are fee-only planners with at least three years experience in comprehensive financial planning; members are also required take 60 hours of continuing education every two years. For referrals to NAPFA members in your area, the toll-free number is 888-333-6659.

◆ **The Licensed Independent Network of CPA financial planners (LINC)** at 800-737-2727, for referrals to fee-only planners who are also CPAs.

◆ **Charles Schwab's AdvisorSource** (800-777-3337). AdvisorSource is a list of some 450 advisers who act as portfolio managers for clients with at least $100,000 of investable assets. To make the list, a financial planner must have at least $25 million under management, five years of money management experience, and a four-year college degree or a Chartered Financial Analyst designation (*see below*)—or 10 years of money management experience without the degrees—and a clean disciplinary record. These advisers pay Schwab $2,000 per quarter to participate in the program.

◆ **The International Association for Financial Planning** 800-945-4237. The IAFP is the nation's largest financial planning association. Membership is open to anyone in financial services.

Other designations:

◆ **Chartered Financial Analyst (CFA)**. CFAs typically only manage portfolios, taking clients with at least $100,000 of investable assets. Many CFAs have much higher minimums. The designation, issued by the Association for Investment Management and Research, is held mainly by institutional money managers and securities analysts.

◆ **Chartered Financial Consultant (ChFC)**, a designation issued by the American College in Bryn Mawr, Pennsylvania, to life insurance agents who have completed a financial planning course and passed an exam. A ChFC's recommendations typically will emphasize insurance products and services. You can get referrals from the American Society of CLU and ChFC (800-392-6900).

◆ **Registered investment adviser**. By federal law, anyone who gives specific investment advice to more than

15 clients must register with the Securities and Exchange Commission. But don't be too impressed; the only requirement is to pay a $150 fee. SEC registered investment advisers need no special training and don't have to pass an exam. (Some states do test investment advisers, but these exams focus on knowledge of state laws and regulations, not on investment management expertise.)

To register as an investment adviser with the SEC, an applicant simply pays the fee and files Form ADV. Part I of Form ADV discloses any lawsuits or arbitration proceedings the adviser has been involved in, and any past disciplinary action against him or her by regulators. Part II discloses the adviser's educational background, the type of services offered, and how he or she is compensated.

Any affiliations with financial services companies also must be disclosed on Part II—and you should be aware of them. Tax accountants and stockbrokers, for example, are increasingly forming alliances in states that allow it. (Twenty-six states do not.) In a typical arrangement, the brokerage splits its commissions and fees with the accountant who sends business its way.

**NOTE:** Registered investment advisers are required to provide prospective clients with a copy of Part II of Form ADV. They're not required to disclose Part I, but it is a public document and you can get a copy from the SEC *(see "Appendix")*.

**NOTE:** Stockbrokers, insurance agents, attorneys, and accountants aren't required to register as investment advisers because the SEC considers investment advice to be incidental to their other services.

Before looking for a financial planner, decide what type of advice you need. This book should help. You may want anything from a couple of hours of counseling about a specific problem or situation to a comprehensive investment plan.

From friends, colleagues, and the resources above, get referrals to several candidates. Telephone them to find out more about their credentials and fees. Then make an appointment to meet the two or three most promising candidates.

You should know in advance whether there's a fee for this initial meeting and what ground the meeting will cover. People who are paid on an hourly basis for advice rarely give free advice. Typically, your first meeting is free, but it serves only as an introduction: You describe your situation and what kind of help you're looking for, and the financial planner tells you about his or her background, credentials, and fee structure. Some financial planners cover all these preliminaries in a telephone conversation; then if you decide to schedule a meeting, the planner will charge for it—but will also give you substantive advice pertinent to your situation.

In your first conversation, you should expect a good adviser to ask you questions and listen to what you have to say. Be wary of anyone who gives you a sales pitch rather than asking you for information about yourself. You should also expect the adviser to raise questions and issues beyond the ones that brought you to him or her. Part of a good financial planner's job is to identify problems you haven't seen yourself.

Finally, consider how comfortable you are with this person—and how comfortable he or she is with you. "A good professional should tell you when you're being unreasonable, but he shouldn't try to impose his value judgments about lifestyle and financial goals on you," says Larry Elkin, a financial planner in Hastings-on-Hudson, New York. "His job is to help you sort out your priorities and figure out what's most important to you."

Among the questions to ask:

◆ **What's your educational and professional background?** Most financial planners started in another financial discipline, like insurance or tax accounting, or money management.

◆ **What's your particular strength, your favorite area of personal finance, your investment philosophy?** Find a planner whose skills and interests are a good fit with your main concerns.

◆ **Please describe your typical client.** This is important: You want to avoid being an adviser's biggest client, since that may mean the issues you care about are outside the scope of his or her experience. You also want to avoid being one of the smallest clients, for the same reason. An adviser who deals with extremely wealthy clients will know relatively little about funding a college savings plan and determining eligibility for financial aid, for example.

◆ **Are you a registered investment adviser?** May I have a copy of your Form ADV?

◆ **Do you recommend specific investments?** Do you implement the financial plans you draw up? Will you calculate my investment portfolio's rate of return after fees and expenses?

◆ **Will you send me research reports or newsletters?** Can you show me a sample client statement or financial plan?

◆ **How do you charge?** Do you charge separately for financial planning, implementation, annual review, and portfolio management? What range of fees do you charge for each service? Do your fees cover the times I might call and ask you questions over the telephone, or will you bill me separately for telephone calls?

◆ **What percentage of your income comes from fees, and what percentage from commissions?**

You should also ask for references from clients. Naturally, you'll be referred only to satisfied clients—but you'll learn something from asking what they like best and least about this financial planner. You'll also get a sense of how much their primary financial concerns resemble your own.

## TAX ACCOUNTANTS

 MOST PEOPLE FIRST TURN to a tax adviser for help with their income tax returns. But it's a good idea to maintain this relationship year-round so that you'll have someone to consult before making decisions with tax consequences—and someone to keep you abreast of changes in tax law.

Many income tax preparers are not licensed. It isn't illegal to earn a living preparing income tax returns without a license; remember, it's the taxpayer who is legally responsible for the income tax return—not the tax preparer. (That's one reason why you should never use a tax preparer who advises you to sign a blank income tax return to be filled in later.)

For tax advice from a licensed practitioner, look for a Certified Public Accountant who specializes in taxes, or a tax lawyer, or an Enrolled Agent. CPAs and tax lawyers are licensed by the states they practice in, and Enrolled Agents are federally licensed.

A CPA must pass a comprehensive, nationally administered test and be approved by a state accountancy board. But don't assume that any CPA is a tax expert. CPA training and examinations focus on reviewing and certifying the financial statements of businesses, not on personal income taxes. Call the American Institute of CPAs (201-938-3000) and ask to be referred to members of its tax section—only about 15 percent of the total membership.

To find an attorney who specializes in taxes, call your local bar association.

An Enrolled Agent must pass a rigorous two-day Treasury Department test on tax law. Practitioners who pass the test—only 25 percent of those who took it in 1996—are entitled to represent you before the IRS. For referrals, call the National Association of

Enrolled Agents (800-424-4339). Its members must also complete 24 hours of classroom work annually and adhere to a code of ethics.

A CPA or a tax lawyer will charge higher hourly fees than an Enrolled Agent, and may have more expertise than you need, especially if your tax return is fairly simple and straightforward.

Don't try to schedule interviews with prospective tax accountants during tax season. When you do talk to them, ask them about their credentials and experience. What percentage of the accountant's practice do personal income taxes and estate taxes represent? How much will your tax return cost? Does this tax preparer charge extra to represent you before the IRS if a return he or she prepared is audited—and if so, how much?

## LAWYERS

LEGAL PRACTICE IS EXTREMELY specialized today. When you ask friends, colleagues, your other professional advisers and professional trade associations for referrals to attorneys, make sure that you specify the type of legal advice you need. Estate planning, marital law, bankruptcy, small business, taxes, and real estate are all considered different areas of specialty, although some of them overlap.

Call your local bar association for referrals. Other sources of information:

◆ **The American Academy of Matrimonial Lawyers in Chicago** (312-263-6477) will refer you to divorce lawyers in your area. Its members must have at least 10 years experience in divorce law, which must constitute 75 percent of their practice. They are also required to pass an oral and written examination that includes tax questions.

◆ **The National Academy of Elder Law Attorneys** in Tucson (520-881-4005) can refer you to lawyers in your area who specialize in all aspects of the law relating to elderly people and to disabled people of any age. You should also check your local agency for the aging, which often has arrangements with local attorneys and law schools to provide legal services for low-income older people.

Ask attorneys how many years of experience they have in the area that interests you and what percentage of their practice it represents. As with any professional adviser, you should look for evidence of continuing education. Have they published articles or books? Do they actively participate in the section of the local bar association dealing with their specialties—by conducting educational seminars for other attorneys, for example?

Ask whether the attorney charges a fee for the first consultation and if so, how much it is; and ask how much work is likely to be involved in meeting your needs, and what it will cost. Lawyers charge $150 to $200 or more an hour, depending on where they work and the size of the firm.

The better prepared you are to ask questions relevant to your situation, the more productively you'll use your lawyer's time. One inexpensive way to get up to speed is to visit the Nolo Press Internet site (www.nolo.com), which offers self-help information about a wide variety of legal topics.

It's also worth asking the lawyers you interview if some of what you need to have done can be handled by associates or paralegals, whose time costs less than that of partners.

## STOCKBROKERS

IN MOST CASES, YOU NEED a broker's services to buy individual stocks and bonds. Although some brokers are very knowledgeable about investing, they earn a living by selling financial products, not advice. Many people think brokers share in the investor's gain or loss on the products they sell, according to a 1996 consumer survey. This isn't true; a broker's commission in no way depends on how the investment performs for you.

Brokers are registered representatives, which means they've passed a series of National Association of Securities Dealers tests. There's no financial planning component to these tests; they focus on securities laws. Stockbrokers aren't required to register as investment advisers because as far as the Securities and Exchange Commission is concerned, investment advice is incidental to their main job, which is selling products. (The securities firm itself typically is a registered investment adviser.)

There are two types of stockbroker: Full service brokers earn commissions based on what they sell; their commissions are higher for some products than others. Discount brokers are paid a salary instead of commissions.

You pay more at a full service brokerage because your commissions cover the cost of personal service and advice about what to buy and sell and when to do it. Full service firms have research departments that analyze and recommend stocks; their brokers, often called financial consultants, are assigned to individual clients, whom they will telephone with investment ideas.

In most cases, I don't think these ideas are worth the extra cost of doing business with full service firms.

First, their stock recommendations are less than objective: Full service firms earn huge corporate finance fees from the very same companies whose stock their research departments recommend. Second, in view of how brokers are paid, their own financial needs can easily conflict with yours. Indeed, brokers often pay little attention to their clients' needs: A 1996 study by Prophet Market Research & Consulting of San Francisco that used "mystery shoppers" posing as first-time investors examined the sales practices of 21 of the nation's biggest full service firms. It found that many brokers recommended stocks to these clients without asking basic questions about their tax brackets, income level, or risk tolerance.

The growing consumer preference for paying fee-for-service and buying no-load funds isn't lost on full service brokerage firms. Many now offer fee-based wrap accounts featuring a selection of investments, sometimes including no-load mutual funds. For an annual fee ranging from 1 to 3 percent of the assets in your account, the broker chooses investments for you and manages the account. The fee covers transaction costs. The minimum wrap account size typically is $100,000. (*Note:* Mutual funds offered in wrap accounts, including no-load funds, typically have higher annual expenses than the same funds sold outside wrap accounts.)

If you want a full service broker, get recommendations from friends and other professional advisers. Call your state securities department *(see "Appendix" for a list of numbers)* or the National Association of Securities Dealers (800-289-9999) and ask for the Central Registration Depository reports on the brokers you've been referred to. The CRD is a computer database that gives the educational background and employment history of anybody registered to sell securities, as well as a record of their past legal or regulatory problems, if any. (The NASD will report your inquiry to the broker, but state regulators won't.)

If your candidates pass muster in the CRD, make interview appointments with them. Ask them to describe their backgrounds, experience, investment philosophy, and areas of strength and weakness. Nobody excels at everything. If your main interest is top-rated bonds, you don't want a broker whose passion is small company stocks. Also ask how many clients the broker serves, and the size of his or her typical account.

Tell each candidate how much you have to invest and your goals, and then ask for suggestions. You should also ask each broker to refer you to three satisfied clients—and ask them what they like best and least about the broker.

**NOTE:** *Never* give the broker the authority to buy or sell for you.

If you already know what you want to buy, you don't need a full service broker. Discount brokerages offer a wide range of prices and services. Big discount brokerages like Schwab and Fidelity offer many of same products and services as full service firms. They charge less than full service firms, but often more than twice as much as smaller, no-frills discounters. The American Association of Individual Investors publishes a comprehensive annual guide to discount brokers that details their fees and services (*see "Appendix"*).

**NOTE:** Whether you use a full service firm or a discounter, read all your mail from the broker promptly. If you don't understand something, don't assume it's correct—ask for an explanation. Keep a file of all your correspondence with the broker and a record of all your buy and sell instructions.

## INSURANCE AGENTS

 ANYONE WHO SELLS INSURANCE must be licensed by the states in which he or she does business. Like stockbrokers, insurance agents are paid by commission to sell products, not advice. The insurance agent's commission is included in your premium.

Start by picking the insurance company you want. You can easily comparison shop for term life insurance by calling SelectQuote (800-343-1985), QuickQuote (800-628-3317), and Quotesmith (800-556-9393). These three insurance agencies maintain extensive databases on term life insurance products. They'll quote prices on several policies that all meet your specifications. The information is free; the firms earn a commission if you buy a policy.

For quotes on either low-load insurance or term insurance call USAA Life Insurance in San Antonio, Texas (800-531-8000) and Ameritas Life Insurance in Lincoln, Nebraska (800-552-3553). Both are top-rated insurers that sell directly to the public. (I think you should call USAA and/or Ameritas as a reality check, no matter what policy you ultimately buy; their premiums are a benchmark for good low-priced coverage.) For quotes on low-load life insurance, you can also call Wholesale Insurance Network (800-808-5810), which represents Ameritas and several other direct sellers.

For fully loaded cash value life insurance products, companies that insurance experts cite as better than average are Northwestern Mutual Life Insurance Co., Guardian Life Insurance Co., Massachusetts Mutual Life Insurance, and State Farm Life Insurance. Call them and ask to be referred to agents who represent them in your area.

Identifying good agents isn't easy because the industry's traditional yardsticks—like membership in the life insurance Million Dollar Roundtable, for example—are designed to measure their sales prowess, not their technical knowledge or ethical standards.

Look for a full-time agent who has been in business for several years—not someone who is just starting out. It's very difficult to earn a living on insurance commissions, so there's a huge turnover among agents. Part of what you're paying for is future service; you want to be sure the agent will be there to provide it. Look for designations like CLU (Chartered Life Underwriter) or ChFC (Chartered Financial Consultant), both issued by the American College in Bryn Mawr, Pennsylvania. These indicate that the agent has participated in advanced, continuing training.

A good agent should analyze your insurance needs, clearly explain your options, and also explain why he or she is recommending one option over others. Don't choose anyone you don't understand, no matter how expert he or she seems.

Avoid any agent who implies that life insurance policy illustrations are guaranteed—and never replace one life insurance policy with another without getting a second opinion. Comparison shop for your product by talking to at least one other insurance agent and at least one direct insurer or telephone quote service.

For referrals to fee-only insurance advisers in your area, call Fee for Service (800-874-5662). Fee for Service is a wholesale insurance agency; it sells the low-load life, disability, and annuity products of nine insurers through fee-only advisers. A fee-only insurance consultant earns an hourly rate, will analyze your existing coverage, and if necessary help you find a low-load policy. Three fee-only consultants with national reputations are Glenn Daily in New York City (212-249-9882), Peter Katt in Mattawan, Michigan (616-372-3497), and Elliot Lipson at Horizons Financial Advisors in Atlanta (770-396-4441). CPAs who are Personal Finance Specialists also sometimes offer fee-only insurance consulting or referrals to fee-only insurance consultants. Fee for Service *(see above)* will also refer you to fee-only insurance advisers.

For an expert second opinion on whether a new cash value policy makes sense for you or if a current policy is worth keeping, I recommend an inexpensive service from the Consumer Federation of America Insurance Group (formerly the National Insurance Consumer Organization).

James Hunt, an actuary and director of CFA, estimates the investment return on cash value policy illustrations, compared with the cost of buying a term policy and investing the premium savings in a bank account or mutual fund. Send a policy illustration for coverage you're considering or an illustration of future values (often called an in-force illustration) on a policy you already own to:

CFA Insurance Group
James H. Hunt, CFA/IG
8 Tahanto St.
Concord, NH 03301-3835

The cost is $40 for the first illustration and $30 for each additional illustration that is submitted at the same time. For an analysis of second-to-die policies, the cost is $75 for the first illustration and $30 for each additional illustration submitted at the same time. Send a check payable to CFA/IG, the illustration(s), and an evening telephone number in case Mr. Hunt needs additional information, along with a self-addressed, stamped, business-size envelope.

# Appendix

## INVESTMENT PERFORMANCE BENCHMARKS

THE BENCHMARK THAT BEST FITS your mutual fund depends on how the fund is invested. For example, Morningstar, the Chicago rating service, says the Standard & Poor's 500 Index is the best performance benchmark for 62 of the 113 large-cap growth funds it follows; the S&P 400 Index is a better benchmark for 36 of these 113 funds; and the Wilshire 4500 is the best benchmark for 15 of them.

Below are the most commonly used benchmarks for different asset categories. Ask your adviser which is the best fit for each of your investments or look it up in *Morningstar Mutual Funds,* available at most public libraries.

## U. S. STOCK FUNDS

| | |
|---|---|
| Large Cap Growth | S&P 500 Index; S&P 400 Index; Wilshire 4500. |
| Large Cap Value | S&P 500; S&P 400. |
| Large Cap Blend | S&P 500; S&P 400. |
| Mid Cap Growth | Wilshire 4500; S&P 400. |
| Mid Cap Value | S&P 400; S&P 500. |
| Mid Cap Blend | S&P 400; Wilshire 4500. |
| Small Cap Growth | Russell 2000; Wilshire 4500 |
| Small Cap Value | Russell 2000 |
| Small Cap Blend | Russell 2000, Wilshire 4500 |

## INTERNATIONAL STOCK FUNDS

Morgan Stanley Capital International All Countries (MSCI-AC) World Index; MSCI World Index ex U.S.

## DIVERSIFIED EMERGING MARKETS FUNDS

MSCI Pacific ex U.S.

## INVESTMENT GRADE CORPORATE BONDS

Lehman Brothers Govt; Lehman Brothers Aggregate

## HIGH YIELD (I.E., JUNK) BONDS

First Boston High Yield Index

## MUNICIPAL BONDS

Lehman Brothers Muni Index

## ADDITIONAL RESOURCES

### FOR INFORMATION ON INVESTING

◆ Morningstar sells both print and software products that analyze and rate mutual funds and variable annuity and life insurance products. *Morningstar Mutual Funds* gives you one page of regularly updated information (including performance record, fees, appropriate benchmarks, and the manager's investment strategy) on each of the 1,500 funds it covers. It costs $425 a year, but is available at most public libraries. A more appropriate version for individual investors is *Morningstar Investor,* a monthly publication that features the same analysis and information but covers only 500 funds and costs $79 a year. *Morningstar Variable Annuity/Life Performance* report provides investment performance and fee information on variable annuities and variable life insurance policies. A single issue costs $45. To order any of these newsletters, or a catalogue of all Morningstar products, call 800-735-0700.

◆ *Value Line Investment Survey* devotes one page of comprehensive, regularly updated information to each of the 1,700 individual stocks it covers, detailing their long-term performance and ranking their prospective appreciation in the 12 months ahead. The newsletter costs $570 a year, and is also available at most public libraries. To order *Value Line Investment Survey* or *Value Line Mutual Fund Survey* (a newsletter that competes with *Morningstar Mutual Funds),* call 800-833-0046.

◆ American Association of Individual Investors. For a $49 membership fee, you get a monthly journal on investing, an annual guide to low-load mutual funds, and the *Individual Investor's Guide to Investment Information,* a useful resource guide. The mutual fund guide costs $24.95 for nonmembers. Other AAII publications include a $4 comprehensive annual guide to discount brokers, including their respective services and fees.

> 625 North Michigan Avenue, Suite 1900
> Chicago, IL 60611
> (312-280-0170 or 800-428-2244)
> (www.aaii.org)

◆ *DRIP Investor* provides a free list of companies that sell their stock directly to the public. Write to:

> DRIP Investor
> 7412 Calumet Ave.
> Hammond, IN 46324

◆ There is also a list of no-load stocks on NetStock Direct's Web site (www.netstockdirect.com).

◆ Call the Securities and Exchange Commission to obtain additional information about your broker:

> Office of Consumer Affairs   (202-942-7040)
> Information Service             (800-732-0330)

◆ Telephone numbers of the state securities agencies that can tell you if a broker is licensed and provide his or her educational background and regulatory history:

| | |
|---|---|
| Alabama | (334-242-2984) |
| Alaska | (907-465-2521) |
| Arizona | (602-542-4242) |
| Arkansas | (501-324-9260) |
| California | (213-736-2741) |
| Colorado | (303-894-2320) |
| Connecticut | (860-240-8230) |
| Delaware | (302-577-2515) |
| District of Columbia | (202-626-5137) |
| Florida | (904-488-9805) |
| Georgia | (404-656-2894) |
| Hawaii | (808-586-2740) |
| Idaho | (208-333-8004) |
| Illinois | (217-782-2256) |
| Indiana | (317- 232-6681) |
| Iowa | (515-281-4441) |
| Kansas | (913- 296-3307) |
| Kentucky | (502-573-3390) |
| Louisiana | (504-846-6970) |

| | |
|---|---|
| Maine | (207-624 8551) |
| Maryland | (410-576-6360) |
| Massachusetts | (617-727-3548) |
| Michigan | (517-334-6200) |
| Minnesota | (612-296-2594) |
| Mississippi | (601-359-6363) |
| Missouri | (573-751-4136 ) |
| Montana | (406-444-2040) |
| Nebraska | (402-471-3445) |
| Nevada | (702-486-2440) |
| New Hampshire | (603-271-1463) |
| New Jersey | (201-504-3600) |
| New Mexico | (505- 827-7140) |
| New York | (212-416-8185) |
| North Carolina | (919-733-3924) |
| North Dakota | (701-328-2910) |
| Ohio | (614-644-7381) |
| Oklahoma | (405-280-7700) |
| Oregon | (503-378-4387) |
| Pennsylvania | (717-785-5177) |
| Puerto Rico | (809-723-8445) |
| Rhode Island | (401-277-3048) |
| South Carolina | (803-734-1087) |
| South Dakota | (605-773-4823) |
| Tennessee | (615-741-3187) |
| Texas | (512-305-8300) |
| Utah | (801-530-6600) |
| Vermont | (802-828-3420) |
| Virginia | (804-371-9051) |
| Washington | (360-902-8760) |
| West Virginia | (304 -558-2258) |
| Wisconsin | (608-266-3431) |
| Wyoming | (307-777-7370) |

SOURCE: AAII

**FOR INFORMATION ON WRITING A WILL, ESTATE PLANNING, AND OTHER LEGAL ISSUES**

Visit the Nolo Press Web site (www.nolo.com) or call 800-992-6656 for a list of its very informative and clearly written legal self-help books and software kits. Among the best: *Plan Your Estate, Simple Will Book: How to Prepare a Legally Valid Will, The Quick and Legal Will Book,* and *The Power of Attorney Book,* all by Denis Clifford, and *Nolo's Everyday Law Book: Answers to Your Most Frequently Asked Legal Questions* edited by Shae Irving. Nolo Press also sells WillMaker, software that lets you create a valid will, health care directives, and instructions for your funeral on a computer.

### FOR INFORMATION ON MORTGAGE RATES

◆ BankRate Monitor provides current interest rates nationwide, by city (www.bankrate.com).

◆ HSH Associates, a publisher of financial data, sells a $20 mortgage-shopping kit that includes dozens of rate quotes, updated monthly. Write to:

> HSH Associates
> 1200 Route 23
> Butler, NJ 07405
> (800-873-2837)  (www.hsh.com)

◆ National Financial News Service provides interest rate surveys (www.nfns.com).

◆ Mortgage Market Information Services provides links to mortgage lenders on the World Wide Web (www.interest.com).

◆ The National Center for Home Equity Conversion provides information on reverse mortgages and counseling services, including a 342-page book, *Your New Retirement Nest Egg* ($24.95); a personal reverse mortgage analysis report ($19) that gives a detailed comparison of up to 12 loan choices tailored to your specific situation; and a list of reverse mortgage lenders and counselors nationwide. The book and personal analysis report together cost $39 plus shipping. To order, call 800-247-6553 or write to:

> NCHEC
> 7373 147 Street, #115
> Apple Valley, MN 55124

## INSURANCE COMPANY RATING AGENCIES

◆ **A.M. Best.** (800-424-BEST or 900-555-BEST). The cost is $2.95 per call and $4.95 for each rating.

◆ **Duff & Phelps.** Ratings are free (312-368-3198).

◆ **Moody's.** Ratings are free (212-553-0377 for up to three ratings per call).

◆ **Standard & Poor's.** Ratings are free (212 208-1527).

## USEFUL IRS PUBLICATIONS

(To order, call 800-829-3676)

| | |
|---|---|
| 1 | *Your Rights as a Taxpayer* |
| 463 | *Travel, Entertainment, Gift, and Car Expenses* |
| 501 | *Exemptions, Standard Deductions, and Filing Information* |
| 502 | *Medical and Dental Expenses* |
| 503 | *Child and Dependent Care Expenses* |
| 521 | *Moving Expenses* |
| 523 | *Selling Your Home* |
| 524 | *Credit for the Elderly or the Disabled* |
| 525 | *Taxable and Nontaxable Income* |
| 526 | *Charitable Contributions* |
| 529 | *Miscellaneous Deductions* |
| 533 | *Self-Employment Tax* |
| 535 | *Business Expenses* |
| 547 | *Casualties, Disasters, and Thefts* |
| 550 | *Investment Income and Expenses* |
| 551 | *Basis of Assets,* explains how to determine the basis of property to calculate taxable profit. |
| 554 | *Older Americans' Tax Guide* |
| 559 | *Survivors, Executors, and Administrators,* provides information on reporting and paying federal income tax due on a decedent's estate, and answers questions faced by survivors. |
| 561 | *Determining the Value of Donated Property* |
| 564 | *Mutual Fund Distributions,* explains the tax treatment of distributions to individual shareholders and how to figure gain or loss on the sale of mutual fund shares. |

## FOR INFORMATION ON RETIREMENT AND RELATED ISSUES

◆ **Social Security Administration** (800-772-1213). Don't hesitate to call Social Security or visit its local office for assistance or answers to specific questions; the staff is patient and helpful. For general information, ask for two free brochures: *Understanding the Benefits* (publication 05-10024), a broad overview of all Social Security programs, including Medicare; and *When You Get Social Security Retirement and Survivor's Benefits: What You Need to Know* (publication 05-10077).

◆ **Health Care Financing Administration.** Call 800-772-1213 for free publications: *The Medicare Handbook* and *Guide to Health Insurance for People with Medicare.* Call 800-638-6833 for specific questions about how Medicare relates to your own situation.

◆ **Choice in Dying**, a nonprofit consumer organization, provides free information on living wills and health care proxies. Write to:

> 200 Varick Street
> New York, NY 10014
> (212-366-5540)

◆ **Pension Rights Center**, a nonprofit consumer organization, provides advice, information, and publications about pensions and related issues, including divorce and survivor benefits. For a free list of publications, send a stamped, self-addressed envelope to:

> 918 16th Street, Suite 704
> Washington, DC 20006
> (202-296-3776)

◆ **American Association of Homes and Services for the Aging**, a trade association, offers a free list of continuing-care retirement communities.

> 901 E.St., NW, Suite 500
> Washington, DC 20004
> (202-783-2242)

◆ **American Health Care Association**, a federation of nonprofit nursing and assisted living facilities, offers free brochures and guides on nursing homes and other long-term-care topics.

> 1201 L. Street NW
> Washington, DC 20005
> (202-842-4444)

◆ **United Seniors Health Cooperative**, a nonprofit consumer organization, publishes information on health care issues affecting retirees.

> 1331 H Street NW, Suite 500
> Washington, DC 20005-4706
> (202-393-6222)

◆ **National Association of Area Agencies on Aging** provides information on state and community agencies that offer services for the elderly.

> 1112 16th Street NW, Suite 100
> Washington, DC 20036-4823
> (800-677-1116)

◆ **The National Academy of Elder Law Attorneys**, a professional association, offers a free brochure on how to choose an elder law attorney and a $25 registry of attorneys around the country.

> 1604 North Country Club Road
> Tucson, AZ 85716
> (520-881-4005)

◆ **Legal Counsel for the Elderly**, a center sponsored by the American Association of Retired Persons, supplies free advice and information on legal issues.

> 601 E Street, NW, Bldg. A, Floor 4
> Washington, DC 20049
> (202-234-0970)

◆ **The National Citizens' Coalition for Nursing Home Reform**, a Washington, D.C.–based nonprofit association, publishes *Nursing Homes—Getting Good Care There*, an excellent book about how to deal with nursing home staff to ensure the best continuing care for a member of your family or a friend who is a patient. Copies cost $15; to order, call 202-32-2275.

# INDEX

## ABOUT BLOOMBERG

**Bloomberg Financial Markets** is a global, multi-media-based distributor of information services, combining news, data, and analysis for financial markets and businesses. Bloomberg carries real-time pricing, data, history, analytics, and electronic communications that is available 24 hours a day and is currently accessed by 200,000 financial professionals in 92 countries.

Bloomberg covers all key global securities markets, including equities, money markets, currencies, municipals, corporate/euro/sovereign bonds, commodities, mortgage-backed securities, derivative products, and governments. The company also delivers access to Bloomberg News, whose more than 400 reporters and editors in 70 bureaus worldwide provide around-the-clock coverage of economic, financial, and political events.

To learn more about Bloomberg—one of the world's fastest-growing real-time financial information networks—call a sales representative at:

| | |
|---|---|
| Frankfurt: | 49-69-920-410 |
| Hong Kong: | 852-2521-3000 |
| London: | 44-171-330-7500 |
| New York: | 1-212-318-2000 |
| Princeton: | 1-609-279-3000 |
| São Paulo: | 5511-3048-4500 |
| Singapore: | 65-226-3000 |
| Sydney: | 61-29-777-8686 |
| Tokyo: | 81-3-3201-8900 |

## ABOUT THE AUTHOR

**Lynn Brenner** is a successful business and personal finance columnist. She has written a popular *Newsday* personal finance column for eight years and is a former senior staff writer at *Institutional Investor, American Banker,* and the *Journal of Commerce.* She has also written for *The New York Times, Working Woman, CFO,* and *Global Investor,* covering the insurance, banking, and mutual fund industries. After responding to thousands of reader queries, Ms. Brenner maintains that people need to ask the right questions to get the information they need. In addition to her experience as a columnist, she is the author of *Building Your Nest Egg With Your 401(k)* and *How to Get Your Money's Worth in Home and Auto Insurance.* Ms. Brenner lives in New York City with her husband and daughter, and writes the 401(k) column for *Bloomberg Personal* magazine.